ALSO BY JEFF CRAWFORD

*Inage of God – From Who You Are To
Who You Can Become,* Xulon Press

On A Ship To Tarshish

GOD'S WILL, YOUR LIFE

JEFF CRAWFORD

CROSSBOOKS
PUBLISHING

CrossBooks™
A Division of LifeWay
1663 Liberty Drive
Bloomington, IN 47403
www.crossbooks.com
Phone: 1-866-879-0502

First published by CrossBooks 04/19/2011

ISBN: 978-1-6150-7779-3 (sc)

Unless otherwise indicated, Bible quotations are taken from The English Standard Version of the Bible. Copyright © 2002 by Crossway Bibles, a division of Goodnews Publishers.

Printed in the United States of America

This book is printed on acid-free paper.

Any people depicted in stock imagery provided by Thinkstock are models, and such images are being used for illustrative purposes only.

Certain stock imagery © Thinkstock.

For Mom and Dad,
Thank you for handing me the Christ Candle,
so that my steps would always be ordered
in front of me.

CONTENTS

FORWARD

One of my greatest delights is the privilege given to me in writing the forward for this book, *On A Ship To Tarshish—God's Will, Your Life.*" Before I give some thoughts about this book, I must give you some thoughts on its author, Dr. Jeff Crawford. A book means little to nothing to me if the author's life is not illustrative of the content he has written. Let me assure you, this author and his book are congruent in every way.

I have known Jeff for many years. I have watched him grow into strong manhood and great faith. I have seen him grow spiritually and professionally. I have seen his strength intellectually kiss his personal humility. When I think of Jeff, I think of Julie. I know Jeff and Julie Crawford very well. I love them and have absolutely the highest respect for them. I think of one phrase when I think of Jeff: *"Scholarship On Fire!"* While I have high regard for his intellectual prowess, I have more appreciation for his fire for Jesus Christ.

As he writes about an ongoing struggle in all of our lives, he does so in a highly biblical and creative way. Through sharing some incredible insights about Jonah and his story, we learn wonderful insights on the will of God. After reading about Plan A and Plan B, you will never look at those terms in the same way again. As you look through the chapter titles alone, you will desire to get into this book very soon.

Therefore, if you are ready to know more about the will of God for your life, begin this journey now. If you are ready to see an author unfold a biblical story and lead it to intersect with your life, move on to Chapter one right now. Enjoy the journey to discovering God's perfect will for your life.

Dr. Ronnie W. Floyd
Senior Pastor, Cross Church
December 2010

PREFACE

Not all books are born the same way. My first book, *Image of God*, was born out of a lifetime of mulling over various thoughts and ideas as they related to the Christian life. In some ways that book was a unique task in that I wanted to see if I could even do it. The book you are holding in your hands was born out of a single sermon that I preached on February 1, 2009.

I began my preaching calendar that year with a sermon series called *Amazing Stories*. I wanted to do a series of teachings on the fantastic stories of the Bible, the ones that defy imagination and skeptics write off as myth. I felt that there was something great to be learned in these stories about God, about us, and about how we relate to the Divine. We looked at outlandish stories of the sun stopping in the sky, talking donkeys, and seas that divide. Of course the age-old tale of Jonah being swallowed by, and living in the belly of a whale made the list.

For years I have made it a habit of asking my wife to grade my sermons after I preach them. Julie has heard more of my preaching than anyone. She's been with me since virtually the beginning. She can tell when I'm *on* and when I'm *off*. She is an excellent critic because she wants nothing but the best for me and she knows that I set a high standard for myself when it comes to my preaching. After my February 1, 2009, sermon called *The Deadliest Catch*, Julie's "grade" came with a surprising caveat, "That is your next book." "Really?" was my response. I've known many pastors who modeled their books after whole sermon series, with one chapter representing one weekly message, but I had never considered modeling a whole book after just one 35-minute sermon. And I certainly had not considered writing a book based on this one particular sermon about Jonah and the whale. But Julie was insistent. The sermon really wasn't about Jonah and the whale as much as it was about God and man and specifically about God's will for each of us.

So I took my wife's advice, as I have learned to do on many an occasion these last 19 years. It would take time, however, for the book to come to fruition. My first duties are being a family man and a pastor. Both of these keep me busy enough. I did file my notes away and over the course of the next year I let the thoughts of how I would flesh a manuscript out percolate in my head. Finally, in the spring of 2010, I decided it was time. I needed to either write the manuscript or move on to something else. Writing is a unique endeavor; it takes concentrated disciplined over an extended period of time. I knew that if I didn't make it happen, it wouldn't happen. So I set a writing goal and the real work began. What you are holding in your hands is the end product.

Books are also not born alone. It would be nice to say that I did this all by myself but I did not. To begin, I have a wonderful church that allows me the flexibility to order my schedule. I spend most of my morning hours during the week studying and writing for sermons, various teaching opportunities, etc. The time to write this book fit in that window. My staff is second to none and in the fall of 2010 they picked up some extra duties to free me as I raced down the home stretch with the manuscript. I love these men and women and it is a privilege to serve the Kingdom together with them. A special shout out to Scott Ward for his fantastic work on the cover design for this book. His God-given talent with graphics captured perfectly the image I had in mind when I wrote the manuscript. And two women in particular deserve note. I grant a big word of thanks to Jennifer Baltz for serving as a proofreader for the manuscript. Writing is half of the equation, editing is other half, and in some ways more difficult. Then I must thank my wife, Julie. She was there on the front end with the suggestion and encouragement to pen the book, and she was there at the end to read, and re-read, and yet, read again the manuscript. She was involved in proofing, discussing content, sentence structure, and many other aspects of the document. Thank you, Julie, for standing by me, with me, and for me all of these years.

Foremost there is God. Any deficiencies you find in this book belong to me. Any truth, insight, or "light-bulb" moments all belong to God. Without Him I am nothing, and neither are you. Which answers the "why" of this book. God has a plan for your life. It is a beautifully scripted journey, a voyage of sorts, with you and Him at the helm. "What is God's will for my life?" That is the question this book endeavors to answer. Happy sailing....

Dr. Jeff Crawford
January 2011

CHAPTER 1 –
THE STORY OF YOUR LIFE

"Daddy, tell me a story tonight!"

These are the words of my youngest son, Grayson, as he leaps onto my back for his nightly piggy-back ride up the stairs to get tucked into bed. He is eight years old and full of life and energy. As much as he likes to be told a story when it's time to go to bed, I think (and hope) he enjoys just having some one-on-one time with Dad. Of course, he probably likes delaying the inevitable too!

My ritual with Grayson goes like this: as we approach the top of the stairs with him clinging to my back, I reach around and start to tickle him. He knows this is coming and he starts to giggle and scream before I even touch him. He jumps off my back as soon as we arrive on the landing, then he runs into his room, turns off the light, and jumps into bed, mummifying himself in his covers. The light has to be off for story time, that's important. I then lay down next to him and he snuggles up to me. I ask, "What kind of story do you want tonight?" Through the years, I have told all kinds of stories – stories about when I was a kid, fantastic stories that I make up out of my head, and of course, stories from the Bible.

Grayson's favorite stories are, hands down, the stories from God's Word. If you think about it, the Bible has everything to capture the imagination of a child, especially a young boy. There are battles with people getting their heads cut off. There are "unbelievable" stories of the sun stopping in the sky and the sea parting. Stories with fire falling from heaven and burning up the bad guys. There are even stories with hailstones the size of cars falling from the sky. Stories about demons and angels. Stories about heroes and villains. And a grand story about the greatest hero of all time, being slain, and coming back to life, with the future story of his promised return on a white horse, riding out of heaven with sword in hand. Man, what kid wouldn't love this stuff?

TRUE STORIES

Here's the kicker about these stories from the Bible, and I always stress this to Grayson - these stories are *true*. They really did happen. These aren't myths or legends, they are fact. No matter how marvelous or fantastic or unbelievable they might seem, these things really did take place. Grayson just stares at me with wonder in his eyes. I think that is why he wants to hear the stories from the Bible, they trump anything from the mind of man.

The Bible is a lot of things. It is God's Word: perfect, inerrant, and infallible. The Bible is trustworthy in all the things to which it speaks. The Bible is a book of theology and doctrine. It tells us about God: His nature, works, and ways. It tells us about ourselves: our sinful nature, our sinful works, and our sinful ways. And it tells us about Jesus who can save us from ourselves and reconcile us to God. You can base your life on the Bible. It is authoritative. In fact, it is *the* authority for your life.

For all that the Bible is as described above, it is also something else - it is a Story Book. And I would argue that before the Bible is any of the other things listed above, it is first and foremost a Story Book. Isn't that how most all of us first encounter the Bible, as a story? My earliest recollection of church and the Bible is of the stories I learned.

The story of Moses parting the Red Sea.

The story of David and Goliath.

The story of Joshua and walls of Jericho.

The story of Jesus.

You get the idea. It's about the stories.

Stories are powerful. They capture our attention and pull us in. They teach us without us even knowing we are learning something new. Have you ever noticed that Jesus' preferred method of teaching was storytelling through parables? Do you remember the points from the sermon preached last Sunday? Probably not, but I'll bet you remember some story the pastor told. You see my point, don't you? Story equals power. I think it's interesting that in this day and age of technology, with all the gadgets that vie for our attention, the ones that capture us are the ones that tell stories.

Consider Netflix. I learned just the other day, that in the evenings, Netflix is responsible for 20% of the bandwidth being used on the Internet. That is amazing to me. What's the deal with Netflix? It's all about the story. People are watching movies, which are nothing more than moving picture stories.

Consider Amazon's Kindle. The Kindle is just one of many e-readers that have come to market, but it is by far the leader. Amazon won't disclose sales figures, but USAToday has reported that e-book sales for 2010 were near $1 billion, with 17.6 million people on the bandwagon.[1] What's the deal with the Kindle and other e-readers? It's about the story.

Technology might make paperbound books obsolete, but the story will never be obsolete.

This means that the Bible will never be obsolete. Its stories have captured the attention of children and adults for millennia. Just walk down the street today and ask a ten-year-old who Moses is and he will most likely know. "Oh yeah! That's the guy with the long beard who parted the sea. The guy with the Ten Commandments." The kid may not go to church or know any of the Ten Commandments, but he knows the story.

That's what the Bible is - a collection of stories. Not just any stories, but stories about God entering into and working in the lives of people. But the Bible is something more, and this is the part that many people miss: the stories of the Bible work together to tell a larger Story, a mega-Story. I call it The Story of God. You see, God is doing something with His creation. He has a plan, and that plan involves real people.

People like your spouse.

People like your children and parents.

People like you.

WHEN GOD'S STORY MEETS YOUR STORY

The Bible is a Story about God and people. Your life is a story too. This book is about how God's Story intersects with the story of your life; and how when that happens, God's Story becomes your story as well.

Each and every day you are adding words and pages to the story that is your life. Have you ever read a biography? It is the written account, or the story, of someone's life. I am a huge C.S. Lewis fan. I have read many of his books from his fictitious *Chronicles of Narnia* series to his more serious works like *Mere Christianity*, *The Great Divorce*, and *A Grief Observed*. I have always been fascinated with the writings of Lewis and with the man Lewis. Because of this, I also have in my library a biography by Alan Jacobs called, *The Narnian*. It is a wonderful book that tells the story of the man behind all the stories and writings.

While no one has probably ever written a biography about your life, and while you probably will not ever pen an autobiography, your life is nevertheless a story. As a pastor I have preached at many funerals. A common element at every funeral I have done is the telling of stories of the life of the one who has died. People come to funerals who are acquainted with the deceased on various levels. They come to remember and to mourn. And that is why the telling of stories is important. I always find out things that I never knew about someone at their funeral. I hear stories about the person who died that deepens for me my understanding of who they really were.

Even the shortest of lives is a complete story. One of the great griefs of my ministry was the funeral of a little boy in our church last year named Collin. Collin was born in early 2008, and when he was seven months old he was diagnosed with Acute Myeloid Leukemia. Collin underwent three rounds of chemotherapy at Arkansas Children's Hospital, all before his first birthday. His parents, Philip and Emily, spared nothing to treat their only child, moving to San Antonio, Texas and renting an apartment so they could be next to the Texas Transplant Institute where Collin was given a cord blood transplant. Collin would eventually develop Stages 3 and 4 graft-versus-host disease of the skin. The complications of the GVHD would go on to claim Collin's earthly life in May of 2010.

In a limited way, that is the story of Collin's short life. But his story goes much deeper and further. At his funeral were told all the stories, and displayed were Collin's favorite toys. I know that he loved to ride his red tricycle up and down the halls of the hospital. He was an accomplished finger painter and a big fan of Elmo. He was brave and fearless and would show you with his little index finger who was #1. He was loved by his church who followed his story and prayed for him. But he was loved most dearly by his parents who miss him so much.

You have now read just a very short version of Collin's story, but there is so much more. His mother, Emily, has written a biography of sorts on the Caring Bridge website with over 300 entries along with photos. So much story in just two short years of life.

You see, we all are walking stories. Your life in particular is a story with, what I want to propose are, two central characters - you and God. Your whole life will eventually be defined by the relationship that you have with God. When your funeral is held, people will gather and they will tell stories. And trust me, the place of God in the story of your life will make all the difference in the world as to the stories that are shared by those who knew you best.

God's Plan (Story) For Your Life

Not only is your life a story, but God has actually drafted the story of your life in advance. In other words, God has a plan for your life. Let's call this Plan A. Plan A is the best of the best that God has for you. I believe that as God's children and unique creations, made in the image of God Himself, He wants nothing but the best for us (Genesis 1:27). But God has also created Man with this thing called freewill. We have the freedom to choose and make decisions for our own lives. God will not force Plan A onto us. If we decide that we want to trek out on our own and go with Plan B, God will let us. The big problem with Plan B is that it's not the best! That's why it is Plan "B." It is a backup, an alternate, a detour, a whole different story than the one God has written for you. The wonderful thing about God, though, is this: while He allows freewill in your life, and lets you wander off and make mistakes, He also offers to you points where you can jump back onto Plan A. So if you get diverted and opt for Plan B only to discover that you blew it, all is not lost. God can and will rescue you. We will see all of this fleshed out in the coming pages.

THE WILL OF GOD

What we are really talking about here is the will of God, specifically the will of God for *your* life. When I teach about this, I talk about two types of God's will: *God's perfect will*, and *God's permissive will*.

God's perfect will for your life is Plan A. It is the story that He has written for you. This story will be unique from anyone else's story. It will be a wonderful life journey with you and God as the main characters. You cannot imagine how awesome and wonderful God's perfect will for your life is and will be. When I reflect on my own life to date (which hopefully isn't even half over!), I am in awe at all that God had planned for me. Because of His plan for my life, I have had the privilege of traveling the world and seeing God work in the lives of people on four different continents. Recently I was able to take my oldest son Garrett with me to Tanzania on a mission trip. It was just incredible. And to think that God's Plan A for my life intersected with His Plan A for my son, and that this was Plan A for both of us while we were in Africa together, is a blessing and memory I will carry with me forever. I promise that you will never be able to plan anything for your life that will out-do God's Plan A, His perfect will.

God's permissive will for your life is Plan B. This is when God lets you set aside Plan A and pursue your own plans and desires. In some cases they may be good plans, maybe even noble plans, but the problem is that they are not the best plans for your life. Let me ask you a question. Would you rather live a good life or the best life that God would have for you? Would you rather eat a delicious seeded watermelon or a delicious seedless watermelon? Now I'm taking for granted that you like watermelon like I do, but I think you get the point. Both watermelons are delicious, but one is the best. So many times we choose to ignore God's best because we have found something good that we think will grow into something better. But it won't.

There are other times that we just plain choose to pursue foolish plans for our lives. Instead of Plan A, it is more important to us to go it alone even though we know it's not the best. We might even trick ourselves into thinking that God does not want the best for us, that He is cruel and has it out for us. So we choose to trust in ourselves and our own plans instead of God. I have seen Plan B lead people to utter and complete ruin. I have seen lives wasted on Plan B. And because people are stubborn, many times they never ever turn back and they ride Plan B all the way to the grave and into eternity.

God's perfect will and God's permissive will are real things. The Bible is full of stories of people who abandoned Plan A for Plan B. It was not God's perfect will for David to sleep with Bathsheba, but God allowed it. He permitted it. It was not God's perfect will for Eve to eat the fruit of the tree of the knowledge of good and evil, but she was tricked into thinking God did not have her best interests in mind, that Plan A was inferior, and so she freely chose Plan B and ate the fruit… and we all know how well that worked out!

FINDING PLAN A

This book is concerned with Plan A - God's perfect will for your life. I do not want you to miss a single page or word that God has drafted for the story of your life. But that brings up a very crucial question, a question that is asked of me all the time: how do I know what God's perfect will for my life is?

I usually get this question when someone comes to me facing a major crossroads in life. Should I take the new job that requires me to relocate my whole family? I have scholarships from two great colleges. Which one do I choose? Should we take advantage of great interest rates and upgrade to a bigger home? Should I go on the mission trip and give up my family vacation? What is God's will?! Each of the above questions has been asked of me at one time or another. Granted, some of these real life examples are more "crucial" than others, but at the time that the question is being asked, it is a big deal in the life of the person asking.

At other times, I get more introspective inquiries from people. "Pastor, I'm just struggling with what God's overall will for my life is." What they are inquiring about is God's direction for their life. They feel that something is not right with their current station in life. Maybe they are just feeling like they're stuck in a rut going nowhere, but know that God must have something better for them. So they wonder what that is: what is God's will for me?

These people all have something in common - they are looking for Plan A, God's perfect will for their life. But they all feel like they can't quite find it. I have seen great frustration among God's people as they seek Plan A, as if it is elusive and hard to find. Then they get frustrated at God, wondering why He makes it so hard. "Why can't my pastor tell me? Why can't I just open my Bible and find the answer? Why doesn't God just give me a Magic 8 Ball to shake and turn over?"

I want to contend in these pages that finding the will of God isn't really that hard or mysterious at all. In fact, being square in the middle of Plan A is a very easy and natural thing to do. It is so easy that most people just miss it. How could this be? How could it feel so hard to find God's will if it is supposed to be easy? Two reasons…

BARRIERS TO FINDING PLAN A

The first barrier to finding Plan A is Plan B. Most people live a good portion of their lives on Plan B. Even Christians. We make so many choices on a daily basis that are based on us and our own desires and comfort rather than based on God's desires and other people. As Rick Warren says in his book, *The Purpose Driven Life*, "It's not about you." But most of us choose ourselves over God or others, and that is always a Plan B choice.

Here is what you need to know: the further down the road of Plan B you travel, the further away Plan A will seem. Most people make the decision to seek Plan A when they come to a major crossroads in life. But since they have walked Plan B for so long, Plan A is virtually indiscernible.

The second barrier to finding Plan A is that we ask the wrong questions. We tend to want a quick fix. "Just tell me which college to go to." "Do I sell the house or not? Tell me now." This is the wrong approach. In order to be in a position to ask this question and receive a clear answer, we need to be asking three other important questions. You see, I have come to believe through my study of God's Word that God's perfect will works according to what I will call the *principle of triangulation*.

THE PRINCIPLE OF TRIANGULATION

The principle of triangulation is simple. Based on the knowledge of three fixed points, you can know where you are. My first generation iPhone had a Maps app. I could press a button and using triangulation, and it would show me on the map where I was located. It did this by using the cellular signal of my phone to locate three cell towers. Those three fixed points would be used to calculate where I was. That's the principle of triangulation.

When it comes to locating Plan A for your life, there are three fixed points, or questions, that you can always ask yourself to triangulate your position. While the big question, "What's God's perfect will for my life?" may be difficult to answer, these three questions are very easy to answer. The answers to these three easy questions will serve to show you if you are currently, right now, walking Plan A or B for your life, and will even give you a sense of how far off track you might be. They will also clearly point the way to Plan A if you are off track. Once you have joined God's Plan A for your life, you will discover that the answer to the big question regarding God's perfect will for your life will come almost naturally to you.

I know what you're saying right now, "Come on Jeff, just give me the three questions!" But a warning first: don't let the simplicity of the three questions fool you as to the power that lies within them, especially when you use them together, applying the principle of triangulation. With that said, here they are:

1. What is my fixation?
2. What is my location?
3. What is my vocation?

That's it. These three simple questions, I believe, are the key. I use them in my own life and have taught others to use them. In the pages that follow, I will break each of them down and apply them for you to see.

ONE STORY, TWO CHARACTERS

The three questions are illustrated in various places throughout the Bible. That is important for you to know. This is not just something I came up with, and this book is not a self-help book. The three questions and the principle of triangulation as it relates to God's perfect will for your life are soundly based in the biblical text.

The clearest representation of this is found in the story of Jonah. I have preached from the Book of Jonah many times, highlighting many different teachings. But I believe the story of Jonah is first and foremost a story about God's perfect will for Jonah. In this story we will see Plan A for Jonah come into conflict with Jonah's own Plan B. We will see the consequences of Plan B and how Jonah got back on track. The principle of triangulation and our three questions are on full display. It is the perfect story to illustrate all that I am talking about.

When most people think about the story of Jonah, they think about Jonah and the whale. Isn't that the way we title the story for kids? Isn't that the way we tell the story at bedtime or at church? But the two main characters of this story are not Jonah and the whale. The two main characters are Jonah and God.

If you are ready to get going, then turn the page and let the story begin...

Q1: *What is your fixation?*

Chapter 2 –
Fixated on God

God and Jonah. That is the story told in the book named for the prophet Jonah. Look at how the story begins:

Jonah 1:1-2
Now the word of the LORD came to Jonah the son of Amittai, saying, "Arise, go to Nineveh, that great city, and call out against it, for their evil has come up before me."

Notice that hints of all three of our triangulation questions are here in these two verses. Jonah is given a "vocation" to perform and a "location" to be. We will talk more about these two points later on, but for now I want us to focus on "fixation."

Let's go back to our first question from the last chapter: *What is your fixation?* Think of fixation as something or someone on which you are focused. Everybody fixates or focuses on something.

I'm a techie. I love the latest and greatest gadgets that come out. When I hear that Apple is going to be introducing a new product, I tend to fixate. I read the "rumor mill" on the Internet. I watch Steve Jobs when he does his media reveal from California. Fixating in this way is not necessarily bad in and of itself, but it can be when you fixate to the detriment of more important things.

I know guys who fixate on video games. They spend all their money and all their time on the newest games and gaming systems. They live to play these games for hours on end. In extreme cases, guys can go without much food (or just a steady diet of pizza) and even simple hygiene like taking showers. They can even ignore more important things like school, work, and relationships. And if the they are married…well, enough said. You get the idea. Fixation can be unhealthy.

We can also fixate on people. During my sophomore year in college at Oklahoma Baptist University, I became fixated on this beautiful new freshman named Julie Dickson. Julie and I first met on the phone. She was a member of the Baptist Student Union and was on a team of college students from OBU working to put together a weekend retreat for high school students in Shawnee. Julie's specific job was to find the retreat speaker. She had actually booked the regional Young Life Director who ended up cancelling on them just a week before the retreat. Another student on the planning team knew about me, that I was called to the ministry, and that I had done quite a bit of speaking at camps and retreats. So Julie called me one evening in my dorm room. That is where the fixation began.

I know this sounds silly, but man, there was just something about her voice. I was hypnotized. And I didn't even know what she looked like! You've probably heard of "love at first sight." Well, this was "love at first sound." Before I knew it, I had agreed to be the speaker for the retreat.

Let me just illustrate for you how powerful fixation can be as it works on us. You see, I am a big Arkansas Razorback fan. Sort of comes from being born and growing up in Arkansas! Well, it just so happened that the Razorbacks were in the Final Four of the NCAA tournament that year. They were scheduled to play Duke in the semi-final matchup (and I just hate the Duke Blue Devils). Guess when the game was scheduled to be played. You got it, during the retreat! So what did I do? Duh, I chose the girl over the game! That's what fixation will do.

I began to ask all my friends if they knew who Julie Dickson was. I just had to see what she looked like. I eventually found her in the cafeteria. And boy, oh boy, did I hit the jackpot. She was gorgeous! My fixation went to a whole new level. We eventually met for a couple of team planning meetings and I was able to shake her hand. It was the most incredible handshake of my life. Julie and I talked more on the phone, probably more than we needed to. The retreat eventually came and went and we got to know each other very well, becoming friends. There is so much more to this story of fixation, but just to bring you up to date, at the writing of this book, Julie and I have been married now for over 18 years. And the story of my fixation with this beautiful, godly woman with the captivating voice continues.

TROUBLED FIXATION

That is fixation. We are, all of us, fixated on various things to various levels at all times. Fixation is natural and normal. It is why we have hobbies and interests and a spouse and children and all the spice that makes life fun. But fixation can also get us into trouble. It does this in one of two ways.

If you do not have a fixation on God and the things of God, you will always, always, *always* find yourself floundering in life with no clear direction or purpose. Remember that the purpose of this book is to help you find God's will for your life. Not His permissive will, but His perfect will. And the first point of triangulation is fixation on God.

The second way fixation can lead you astray is when you allow any other fixation in your life to rise above and supplant your fixation on God. If anything or anyone comes before your God fixation, you will run into trouble and find yourself confused when it comes to God's will. Now hear me clearly - it is not that having other fixations is bad. It is when those other things or people rise above God in importance and attention that they become a problem. In other words, it is not a problem for a teenage boy to have a girlfriend and to fixate on her, but the problem comes when the girlfriend replaces God as his highest level of fixation. Anything or anyone that keeps you from following Jesus and being what God wants you to be is trouble.

Going back to my college fixation with the girl who would one day be my wife - was I highly fixated on her? Yes! But when it came time to focus on the retreat she had invited me to speak at, my fixation on God was my priority. I joked about choosing the girl over the game, but I really did pray over whether or not I should accept the invitation to be the retreat speaker and I felt that God really wanted me to do it. This is a good time to go a little deeper with you regarding my own personal God fixation.

I became a Christian when I was 14 years old, and I was called into the ministry shortly afterward. I will tell you that I was one fixated teenager on God and the things of God. I wanted to live my whole life serving Jesus Christ and the Kingdom. My fixation is what led to my eventual vocation and even location. Once again, I will talk more about these two points later.

It was my fixation on God that led me to Oklahoma Baptist University for my undergraduate work. That put me in the path of the woman that would one day be my wife. On a very small level you can begin to see how these three points of triangulation - fixation, location, and vocation - are key to being in the right place at the right time so that the perfect will of God regarding the BIG things of life (like who to marry) are crystal clear and not something hard or difficult at all.

As I grew and matured in the Lord, I began to have more and more opportunities to travel and speak at a very young age. I preached my first sermon at the age of 16. At the age of 18 I was flying down to Louisiana to preach to over 3,000 teenagers at the Louisiana Baptist State Youth Evangelism Conference. Shortly afterward, I was asked to be the featured speaker at various youth camps in Louisiana. Then, the summer after I graduated from high school, I served as a missionary in Florida as the preacher for a revival team that traveled the state. I preached nine revivals in nine weeks that summer. And I made money. And that is a key point to this story.

I will never forget when I drew my first paycheck for ministry. It almost didn't seem right and it certainly did not feel right. I just could not fathom taking money for doing something I enjoyed so much. But the money was nice, especially as a college kid enrolled in a private Christian college.

Eventually, it became almost expected that I should receive some sort of compensation for preaching. Usually it was only $50 and sometimes less, but it was the expectation of compensation that began to become a new fixation for me.

When Julie approached me about being the speaker for the BSU retreat, she told me that they had no money to pay me. I'd have to do it for free. I remember distinctly standing at a crossroads over this issue. It was one of those "what is

God's will" crossroads. If I took the opportunity to speak at this retreat, not only would I not get paid, but I'd also have to miss seeing Arkansas play in the Final Four. I know all this may sound silly and immature, but remember I was only 19 at the time and I *was* silly and immature. What was in it for me if I did this retreat? Certainly no cash and no ballgame.

It all really came down to fixation. Who would win? God, or gold and the game. Because my fixation on God overrode my fixation on money and the Razorbacks, I accepted the invitation. It was good for me to do something where money was not involved. I needed to be reminded about why God called me into ministry in the first place. As it turned out, Arkansas lost to Duke anyway. I can't help but wonder what if, just what if I had chosen not to listen to God. If I had missed the retreat, would I have also missed the love of my life? Is fixation important? You bet!

JONAH'S FIXATION

When the story of Jonah begins, we see fixation very clearly on display. We are told that "the word of the Lord came to Jonah, son of Amittai." As you read these opening verses of the book, you will notice a couple of things.

First, God was fixated on Jonah. Don't miss this. It's important. God cared about Jonah. Have you ever wondered if God cares about you? You may feel very small in the world, insignificant, like nobody cares. Or you may not be that down on yourself, you just are keenly aware that if you died tomorrow, friends and family would mourn, but most of the world would not notice. After a few weeks, life would go on as normal, even for most of those closest to you. That is life for most people, and it is easy to think that God has more important things and people to concern Himself with other than you.

Read this first verse again from the book of Jonah: "the word of the Lord came to Jonah, the son of Amittai." God was fixated on this man Jonah enough that He had words for him. Can you imagine? The God of all creation wanted to talk to the one He created. Out of all the things happening on the earth that day, God had time and care enough for Jonah. I know what you're thinking, "But this is Jonah, he's a prophet. He's got a whole book of the Bible named after him. He's *important*." Now hold on a second. What do we really know about Jonah?

JONAH WHO?

The answer is: not much. We know that his father was a man named Amittai, which doesn't help much at all. Outside of the actual book of Jonah, there is only one other reference to Jonah in the entire Bible. It is found in 2 Kings 15:17. We learn from this one verse that Jonah was a prophet who lived during the reign of Jeroboam II. This would put the dates of his ministry around 793-753 B.C. Jonah had the privilege of delivering the good news from God that Israel was about to experience a time of safety and prosperity.

That verse also tells us that Jonah lived in a town called Gath-Hepher. The town's name literally means "winepress of digging." It was probably a town with a lot of grapevines, and those who lived there pressed the grapes and sold the wine. Gath-Hepher was just a spit of a town located next to Nazareth, the same Nazareth where Jesus would grow up. From biblical records we know that Nazareth was a very small and insignificant town. It stands to reason that if Nazareth had to be used as a point of reference for Gath-Hepher, then Gath-Hepher must not have been much of anything at all. In Arkansas, we would say that Jonah was "from the sticks." He was a man who lived in the middle of nowhere and who probably pressed grapes for wine to make a living.

The point is this: wherever you live and whatever you do, you probably are more well known and have more friends and family than Jonah did. But for all that Jonah was not, God was still interested in him. God was fixated on him.

The second thing you will notice from reading the opening verses of the book of Jonah is that Jonah was fixated on God. This is a requirement of sorts for any prophet. Prophets hear from God and then they relay God's Word to the people. As already noted, Jonah is mentioned in the book of 2 Kings as delivering a word of good fortune to God's people. This is another clue that informs us that Jonah was fixated on God. I am sure Jonah was fixated on other things as well, perhaps his day job as a grape presser, or his wife and kids (if he had any), etc. But none of these took precedent over his fixation on God.

It was Jonah's fixation on God, along with the other two points of triangulation, that put Jonah in the middle of God's perfect will when the story begins. This is what made it possible for Jonah to hear very clearly about what God's will was for his life: God wanted Jonah to travel northeast over land to the pagan city of Nineveh and deliver a prophecy of destruction to the people that lived there. This was God's will for Jonah and Jonah knew it. And we know Jonah heard clearly from God because he immediately got up and went in the opposite direction! Jonah wanted nothing to do with God's perfect will. We'll see how this plays out later on. Suffice it to say for now, that as a pastor, I come across people all the time who claim to be searching for God's will, when in fact they know full well what it is - they just don't want to follow God.

False Fixation

There is one other thing I have learned about fixation and God. This is a word for those who have been Christians for a long time and are "doing" all the right things in life. It is possible to appear to be in the center of God's will doing all the right things, and *think* you are fixated on God when, in fact, you are not.

The perfect example of this is the biblical character of Samuel. What we have in Samuel is the story of a young man who was around God and the things of God from the moment he was born. His mother, Hannah, had been barren but desperately wanted a child. She went before the Lord in prayer and asked Him for a son, promising to give him back to God for His service if only God would open her womb. God granted her request and Samuel was born.

After Samuel was weaned, Hannah kept her promise to God and presented him before the Lord in the temple to the priest Eli. Eli would rear Samuel, who would eventually become one of the greatest prophets in Jewish history. Two whole books in the Bible bear Samuel's name and tell of his exploits during the times of King Saul. Samuel was truly a remarkable man whose life was characterized by an intimate fixation on God and footsteps squarely in the middle of God's perfect will.

But early in his life, we see an episode where Samuel suffered from false fixation. Imagine growing up as a young boy around a bunch of old priests with the temple of God as your playground. Sounds like fun, huh? You would think that it would be impossible for Samuel to not be focused on God. By all accounts, Samuel was a good boy who did everything right.

Eli had sons of his own, but in contrast to Samuel they did everything wrong. In fact, the Scripture tells us that they were "worthless." As sons of Eli, who was a priest, these boys would have naturally been in line to be priests themselves. But they were clearly not interested in the will of God for their lives. Their exploits went as far as seducing and having sexual relations at the entrance to the tent of meeting with the women who came to serve God! So it is definitely possible to be around God and the things of God and have no interest or fixation on God.

But this was not Samuel. He towed the line. He was the son Eli wished was his own and that Eli would view as his own. Eli loved Samuel and did all he could to nurture Samuel and train him for the priesthood.

When we see Samuel in the third chapter of the book of 1 Samuel, he is in the right place (geography) doing all the right things (vocation). It would make sense that he would be properly fixated on God. But he was not. We are told that late one night he was awakened from his sleep by God. In other words, the word of the Lord came to Samuel, just like it did Jonah. But Samuel did not recognize the voice of God. Instead, Samuel got up from his bed and went to wake up Eli, who he *thought* was calling him. "Here I am!" said Samuel. Note the enthusiasm in his voice. This was a great kid, ready to go and do anything for God no matter the time of night.

Of course, Eli didn't call Samuel and probably thought the boy was having a vivid dream. He sent Samuel back to bed. God then woke Samuel up a second time. And we have a repeat. Samuel woke up Eli, and Eli sent him back to bed, probably a little perturbed about losing sleep because of an overanxious boy.

God called to Samuel a third time. By now you know the routine. Except this time Eli was starting to figure out what was going on. When he sent Samuel back to bed this third time, he gave him some additional instructions. "Listen, Samuel, when you hear this voice the next time, *don't come and wake me up.* Instead, just answer back, 'Speak, Lord, your servant hears.'" I can just see Samuel shuffling back to bed after this third time, "Crazy old man, he keeps calling for me in his sleep and he doesn't even know it. What does he want me to do, talk to the walls?" But Samuel obeyed. That was always a positive about Samuel - he was willing to obey authority whether or not it made sense.

Sure enough, God called to Samuel a fourth time, and per his mentor's instructions, he replied to God, "Speak, Lord, your servant hears." Finally, God was able to get Samuel's attention and have the conversation He had been trying to have with him all night.

You see, Samuel is the perfect example of someone who was always in the right place at the right time doing all the right things, except that he was so ready to do anything *for* God that he wasn't ready to hear *from* God.

Could this be you? Are you the person who goes to church every single week and has for most of your life? Are you the person who gives to your church both financially and in time doing service? Perhaps you've gone on mission trips or taught kids in Sunday School, or taken vacation time to help with VBS. If your pastor calls, you are willing to do anything and everything for God. But can you hear God? Are you fixated, I mean really fixated, on God? Not some false sense of fixation because you "do" everything by the book. Fixation is so much more. It is your heart's and mind's full and complete attention on God and the things of God. When God calls, you can hear because you are *expecting* Him to speak to you.

This is the kind of fixation we see in Jonah. He was definitely focused on God. He was a successful prophet who had received words from God and had delivered those words to God's people. He was in a state of waiting expectation. Waiting on God to send him another word. And that is exactly what he got in the opening verses of the book of Jonah.

CHAPTER 3 –
AN ISSUE OF WORSHIP

We are all worshippers. And we all worship all the time. Worship is defined as the giving of your heart, soul, mind and strength over to something outside of yourself. You can see that in this way, fixation and worship are linked together.

I am not saying that we worship everything we fixate on. I mentioned that I am a techie; I love the latest and newest gadgets. But I don't worship them. I do, however, know people who fixate to the point of worship. If you are fixating on God to the point of worship, that is the goal! But if you fixate on anything else to the point of worship, you are treading on dangerous ground. What you have done is created an idol.

IDOL FIXATION

Some fixations cry out to be worshipped. I said in chapter one that being fixated on something is not in and of itself a bad thing. I am, to this day, fixated on my wife, and that is a healthy thing. But there are some fixations that are intrinsically evil and should be avoided at all cost. It is never a good thing to fixate on a woman other than my wife!

I identify evil fixation, fixation that should be avoided at all cost, as idol worship. I know what you are thinking. "Idol worship? Come on, not today, not anymore. Idols are a thing of the past or something worshipped in primitive, less sophisticated cultures."

To be sure, physical idols are literally worshipped even today in some third world countries, but they are not limited to ancient history or remote parts of our world. Several years ago I led a mission trip to Buenos Aires, Argentina. Buenos Aires is a mega-city with a population around 13 million people. It is hardly a third world city even though it is not on par with most large cities in the United States.

One day we had our mission team out at a local soccer field interacting with teenagers and playing "futbol." I noticed an unusual area on the outside corner of the field where there were also some picnic tables. I went over to investigate. What I saw was a metal pole about four feet tall cemented into the ground. There was a box about the size of a 20 inch television mounted on top. The box had a locked door on the front, and the door was screened so you could see inside. What was inside? A little statue of a cowboy about 15 inches tall. That's right, a cowboy. Positioned around the cowboy statue were votive candles. Stuffed through the screen and lying around the statue were dozens of pieces of paper with hand written messages from people.

I was not exactly sure what I was looking at, so I asked. I was told it was an idol. The cowboy statue was the representation of an iconic hero in Argentine lore that is literally worshipped today. People bow down in an act of fixated worship and give of themselves, their hopes and dreams, to this idol.

Oh yes, idol worship is alive and well in our world today in some of the most unlikely places. Places like a soccer field on the edge of one of the most populated cities in the world.

American Idols

But not in America, right? Not here.

I'm sure you have never bowed down to an idol, have you? You probably don't know of anyone who has either. But think again. Remember that idols don't exist as objects in and of themselves. Idols always represent some specific fixation.

Time for a little history lesson. If you are a student of the Bible you may recall that God's people, the Hebrews, had constant run-ins with various idols throughout the Old Testament narrative. God, it seems, was constantly warning them to stay away from these idols and the fixations they represent in order to focus and fixate, instead, on Him. Sometimes God's people listened and worshiped God, and that is when life for them was blessed and good. At other times, they ignored God and allowed their hearts and minds to drift away and fixate on a pagan idol. That is when life for them became cursed and difficult. God usually stepped in to discipline and correct His people in order to steer their attention back to Him.

The idols of the Old Testament were varied, and each appealed to a different kind of evil fixation. One of these idols was Artemis, the goddess of youth. She was the symbol of the perfect woman. In the ancient city of Ephesus, a huge temple to Artemis was built, which was later classified as one of the Seven Wonders of the World. Young women venerated Artemis and fixated on her beauty.

Have you ever noticed how we worship "youth" today? We seem to have no end to the methods of holding back the clock: Viagra, breast implants, liposuction, Botox, hair plugs, etc. Just stand in line at any supermarket and look at the magazines. You won't see *Mature Living.* It's all about the young and the beautiful. The goal: be 17 forever. There may be no named statue, but Artemis is alive and well and worshipped in America still today.

Or consider the ancient idol Asherah. She was the goddess of sex. Need I say more? The books of the Kings and the Chronicles are full of stories related to Asherah worship. This form of idol worship involved sexual prostitution within pagan temples. Altars would be set up with Asherah poles mounted next to them. Men would come to the altar, pay a fee, and have sexual relations with a temple prostitute. You can see that this form of "worship" would have been very seductive and tempting for any man.

Once again, today there may be no Asherah pole, but sexual prostitution is alive and well in virtually every city in America. Pornography is pervasive, producing more income than the combined revenues of the four major television networks. There once was a day when you had to go find pornography. Today, pornography will find you. It is common for children in grade school to be exposed to pornography via the Internet. Why is it this way? Because we worship Asherah.

Then there is the idol god, Baal. Baal is the god of money. Baal will make you rich. People in the Old Testament would worship Baal in order to secure financial peace and prosperity. Do we worship Baal today? You bet. On any given Sunday more people will go to a mall than will go to church. If you don't have any money, no problem. Baal will give you free money via this thing we call credit. Why is consumer debt out of control? Because Baal is alive and well even today, and we worship him.

What about Gad? He is the god of luck and chance. I live in the state of Arkansas and we just stumbled over ourselves a couple of years ago because we couldn't get a lottery voted into our state fast enough. Missouri has a lottery. Oklahoma has a lottery. Heck, all the states around us have one. Think of all the money going out of our state. So many Arkansans felt we just had to have one too.

Our city, Fort Smith, just had a big brouhaha several years ago over casino gambling. Fort Smith is a border town to Oklahoma and we have two casinos literally outside our city limits just across the state line. Why not *in* the city? A move was made to jockey with some Indian gaming laws in order to get a casino in Fort Smith. "To keep city dollars in the city," we were told. Why is all of this happening anyway? Because we worship Gad.

You may not have heard of the god Molech before, but he will be familiar to you as well. Molech is the god of child sacrifice. As difficult as it is to imagine, people in the Old Testament would literally kill their own children on the altar of Molech in order to incur blessing on their life. They would bind their own flesh and blood with rope, place the child on the altar, and then slit the child's throat. The body would then be burned. Barbaric and evil was the worship of Molech.

But we don't worship Molech today, do we? Who would ever condone, much less carry out, such a heinous act? But Molech worship is alive and well and right in our own backyard. The altar is no longer a stone slab on a hillside, it is now the womb. And while our children, our own flesh and blood, are still bound by the confines of the womb, they are cut and slashed and ripped to pieces. The remains of their bodies are incinerated by fire. All of this is done with the "promise" of a better life without the burden of rearing a child. Oh yes, we worship Molech. In fact, we have become so good at worshipping Molech that we have sacrificed more of our children since Roe v. Wade than any culture in the history of the world.

This is our fixation.

This is our worship.

These are our American idols.

FIXATED ON GOD: A CLOSER LOOK

In the last chapter I pointed out that God was fixated on Jonah and that Jonah was fixated on God. There is no doubt that Jonah was not an idol worshipper. He worshipped the one true and living God.

How exactly do you get to this kind of fixated worship? What does it look like in real, everyday life? Can we make this something that is a little easier to get our hands around and to live out? The answer is YES. The Bible has fleshed out the fixation and worship of God for us.

In the book of Deuteronomy, God talks about what fixation and worship should look like.

Deuteronomy 6:4–5

"Hear, O Israel: The LORD our God, the LORD is one. You shall love the LORD your God with all your heart and with all your soul and with all your might."

These two verses are called the *Shema* by Jews. The *Shema* is sacred to Jews and embodies what it means to be fixated on God. Jews consider these two verses to be the heart of *all* the Law of God. The word *Shema* is the same Hebrew word as the first word of verse four, "to hear." But this is more than a suggestion, it is a command. The word, "to hear," implies most literally "to obey."

The *Shema* is a call to obedience through worship. Notice that verse five defines worship for us. We should love God with every bit of our heart, soul, and might. That, my friend, is a powerful expression of fixation! When Jesus was asked what the Greatest Commandment was in all of God's Law, he quoted the *Shema* (Matthew 22:37-38). Jesus also quoted the *Shema* in Luke when asked by a lawyer what was the secret to eternal life (Luke 10:25-28). It seems clear that the *Shema* was central to Jesus' teaching and preaching.

Now I want us to look carefully at the important verses that follow the *Shema*.

Deuteronomy 6:6–9

And these words that I command you today shall be on your heart. You shall teach them diligently to your children, and shall talk of them when you sit in your house, and when you walk by the way, and when you lie down, and when you rise. You shall bind them as a sign on your hand, and they shall be as frontlets between your eyes. You shall write them on the doorposts of your house and on your gates.

Notice that verse six tells us that the words of God should be "on your heart." What does that mean? Have you ever run across a friend, someone you've been thinking about recently, and your response to seeing them is something like, "You've been on my heart lately"? Or have you ever felt like God was laying a certain someone "on your heart"? If so, then you are getting at what this phrase means. To be "on your heart" is a phrase of fixation. It means that you think about your friend. But it is more than just a mental exercise. You actually feel for that person. There is a personal, emotional, energy-draining investment when something or someone is on your heart.

The next few verses flesh this out even more for us. Unlike our sanitized Christian culture, Judaism is a very tactile belief system. Have you ever noticed in the Old Testament how, as a part of worship of God, Jews built things like altars and burned things on them like incense? This was a part of worship. It required physical, sweating labor. Then you smelled the sweet aroma of a burning fragrance. The whole sacrificial system is tactile. It is filled with things you can touch and see and smell and hear.

The colors of the priestly robes.

The sound of the baying animal as its throat is slit.

The smell of blood running down the altar.

We have nothing like this in our worship today. Most of our worship is cerebral. Our worship centers are air-conditioned and maintained by a custodial staff that the average church member never sees. We would never burn anything in the church building for fear of violating fire code. Plus burning incense just feels too "new age" for many Christians. And you can forget bringing live animals indoors. When I was a kid, our church held a yearly Easter pageant for the community. It was a big deal. One year someone had the bright idea of bringing a real donkey into the worship center when it came time for Jesus to ride into Jerusalem. Well this donkey did what donkeys do (if you know what I mean). To this day people still talk about the live donkey in church!

Today most of our worship centers around a "clean" and "orderly" service whereby we experience God through music and the preaching of the Word. There is nothing at all bad about this. We are just limiting our worship experience to *one* of our five senses: hearing. One reason I love the Lord's Supper (and most Christians I know feel the same way) is that it employs two other senses: smell and taste. You can smell the grape juice just as you tilt the cup up to drink. And of course you taste the bread and the juice as you consume them. It sort of brings a whole new meaning to the verse, "Taste and see that the Lord is good" (Psalm 34:8).

This is the way that God intended for us to experience and worship Him, with *all* of our senses. That is what verses 6-9 talk about. This is fixation fleshed out in day-to-day life.

The Next Generation

The words of the *Shema* tell us that we are to *teach* the words of God *diligently* to our *children*. These three words are very powerful. A major part of what I do as a pastor is teach. I am constantly preparing material for presentation to God's people. Every pastor has their own style of preaching, and I guess you could classify me as a "teacher preacher." I always endeavor to dig out something for God's people that they have never seen or heard before. One thing I love about teaching is that it makes me a learner as well. What I glean in preparation to teach goes far beyond what I actually end up publicly teaching. In this way, teaching keeps me sharp. I feel like I get more out of my sermons than anyone else!

You should be a teacher of God's Word. This is not an option and it is not limited to those with the spiritual gift of teaching. But you may say, "I am just not a teacher." How you teach is also explained in these verses. First notice the word "diligently." This word implies focus, concentration, and longevity. Anybody can get on a bandwagon for a few weeks or months. But fixation / worship is a life-long pursuit.

The word "children" is the important word here. So you don't have the spiritual gift of teaching? Okay, you may not be cut out to sit in a classroom of adults and lecture them for 30 minutes each week. But what about kids? What about *your* kids or grandkids or nieces and nephews? This is to be the focus of your teaching. You can just see the brilliance of God at work. Worship is not just about you. It is also about the next generation. By focusing on children, God is ensuring that the next generation will be brought along.

I have three blessings from God. Garrett and Grayson are my sons, and Madison is my daughter, sandwiched in the middle. I love my kids more than I could ever put into words. They are a fixation of mine. As a pastor, people ask me from time to time if I want my kids to go into the ministry one day. "Only if God calls them" is my reply. When I am asked what my goals are for my kids, my answer is always the same. When my kids grow up and leave my home, I want them to love Jesus, love his church, and love their family. That covers it all. If my kids love Jesus, love his church, and love their family, I will never worry about the other details of God's will for their lives. Loving Jesus will fixate them properly. And loving the church will always put them in a place where they have a support system.

You see, I am serious about this fixation / worship thing. I truly believe it is the first step toward triangulating all of God's perfect will for my life. I believe it so much that this is what I focus my own children on, and I do this because God has said in the words from the *Shema* that this is how it should be.

God Talk

So *how* do we go about teaching our kids these words of God? The answer is in verse seven. We are to "talk of them." That's right, just talk. I know, it sounds too easy. Yes, it is easy, but it is also hard. It's hard because we forget to be diligent. See how it all ties together?

We are told to talk about the things of God to our children when "you sit in your house." What do you talk about when you are sitting in your house? I think too many parents leave the talk of God and the things of God to just church experiences. That's too bad. If that is you, then you are missing it! Talk to your kids as you go about life in your own home. Eat meals together and pray over the food. Ask your kids what God is doing in their lives. Ask them about school. Talk about what God says about the things they are being taught. Talk to your kids.

These verses tell us to talk to our kids as "we walk by the way." What do you talk about when you drive around town? When someone cuts you off in traffic? When you are trapped in the car for four hours on the way to Grandma's house? What do you talk about after seeing a movie with your kids? What do you talk about when you are fishing with your son or after a dance recital your daughter was in? What do you talk about?

We are told to talk to our kids about God "when you lie down, and when you rise up." Do you pray with your kids at bedtime? Do you tell them a story from the Bible? What is the first thing you say to your kids when they get up? You get the picture, don't you? These verses paint a vivid picture of every facet of life, from morning until night, filled with God talk. I'll ask it again: what do you talk about with your kids?

I don't mean just talking *about* God either, as if He's some distant impersonal force. Your instruction to your children should be based on the biblical principles that come from God. The Bible is God's love letter for His children. There is intimacy in that last sentence. Just like the intimacy you share with *your* children. Don't just talk about God. Teach them real life problem solving and attitudes based on God's principles, using God's own words like kindness, patience, etc.

MEZUZAH ME

Verse eight takes another step forward in fleshing out what it means to fixate your worship on God. We are told to "bind" the words of God on our forehands and between our eyes. What does this mean exactly? Jews took this very literally. A small piece of parchment with the words of the *Shema* written on it would be placed inside a small box. This box would then be tied to the arm or around the head with the box resting on the forehead. This box with the *Shema* inside is called a *phylactery*. Even today while watching video footage on the news of Jews at the Wailing Wall in Jerusalem, you may catch a glimpse of men wearing the *phylactery*.

Verse nine indicates that the words of God should also be written on the doorposts of your house and on your gates. Once again, Jews follow a literal obedience to the Scripture here. Remember, Jewish worship is very tactile, involving all the senses. In this instance Jews use a Mezuzah. This is a tiny metal receptacle containing a parchment with the *Shema* written on it. The Mezuzah is then nailed to the inside doorpost of a Jewish home. It is common practice for Jews to pause on their way out for the day and again when they arrive back home, to think on and even touch the Mezuzah.

Do you see the pictures these verses paint for us? Do you see how fixating on God is fleshed out in day-to-day living? Your life is to be filled from morning to night with God talk. Your kids need to hear you talk about and to God. They need *you* to talk to *them* about God. Your life and home need to be filled with God symbols. Not talismans that have any real power in and of themselves, but symbols. Maybe a necklace you wear or a bracelet with Christian meaning. Maybe Bible verses hung decoratively around your home. Maybe sacred art work. Physical symbols that you can't miss that force you to think on God.

I keep a stash of Mezuzahs in my office. Occasionally a church member will ask Julie and I to come to their new home to offer a prayer of blessing on it. I like to take them a house-warming gift, one of these Mezuzahs. I explain what it is and I pray and bless the home, asking God to always fill the home with His presence.

That is fixated worship fleshed out.

"THESE WORDS"

There is one more thing about the *Shema* that I want you to see. In verse six, God says that "*these words* that I command you today shall be on your heart" (emphasis mine). Exactly which "words" is God talking about? Remember that the *Shema* is considered by Jews to be a summary of the whole Law. When talking about the Law from a Jewish perspective, you are talking about the Torah, the first five books of the Old Testament. Very specifically, the Law was introduced first in the form of the Ten Commandments. If you look back just one chapter in Deuteronomy, to chapter five, you will see a list of the Ten Commandments! It is clear that when the *Shema* refers to "these words," it is talking about the Ten Commandments.

The Ten Commandments get their name from chapter four in Deuteronomy.

Deuteronomy 4:13
And he declared to you his covenant, which he commanded you to perform, that is, the Ten Commandments, and he wrote them on two tablets of stone.

In this verse the Hebrew phrase for Ten Commandments is *aseret he'devarim*. The word *aseret* is correctly translated *ten*. But the word *he'devarim* is most accurately translated as the word *sayings* or *declarations*. This is an important distinction. What we have given to us from God are the Ten Declarations. God is telling us that this is the way it is. It does not matter if we like or not, this is Truth.

Take a look at the Ten Declarations and you will see that the first four are all about God (they are listed in Deuteronomy 5:6-15):

1. "I am the LORD your God, who brought you out of the land of Egypt, out of the house of slavery."

Most Christians believe that the First Commandment is "You shall have no other gods before me." But to a Jew, the First Commandment (or Declaration) begins one verse earlier. "I am the LORD your God." Now that is a statement of declaration! God is telling us who He is and who we are. And it is clear where our fixation should be. If there is no God and there is no authority, then *why* the other nine commandments?

2. *"You shall have no other gods before me. You shall not make for yourself a carved image, or any likeness of anything that is in heaven above, or that is in the earth beneath, or that is in the water under the earth."*

As I said, Christians tend to divide the above into two commandments, but Jews view these together as the Second Declaration of God. God has already declared that He is the one and only God, and that He has linked Himself to us. Now we see a declaration that there are to be no other gods in our lives competing with the one true and living God. Once again we see an intense fixation that God requires of us on Himself.

3. *"You shall not take the name of the LORD your God in vain, for the LORD will not hold him guiltless who takes His name in vain."*

Our fixation on God should be holy and righteous, not flippant or irreverent. When our culture fixates on God, it does so by painting a false identity of Him. Names mean something. Elvis. Madonna. Apple. ESPN. Playboy. Ford. Something as simple as a name creates an image of identity for the one hearing the name. It is no different with God. His name is Yahweh. God is a certain kind of God and He demands respect.

4. *"Remember the Sabbath day, to keep it holy. Six days you shall labor, and do all your work, but the seventh day is a Sabbath to the LORD your God. On it you shall not do any work, you, or your son, or your daughter, your male servant, or your female servant, or your livestock, or the sojourner who is within your gates. For in six days the LORD made heaven and earth, the sea, and all that is in them, and rested the seventh day. Therefore the LORD blessed the Sabbath day and made it holy."*

God knows we have other fixations that occupy our time and life: work, family, school, hobbies, etc. And other fixations, as long as they are not idolatrous and evil, are not bad in and of themselves. But when they push God out, they become something unholy. It has been said that "when you take a good thing, and make it a god thing, it becomes a bad thing." The Sabbath is God's way of keeping us fixated on Him, of making sure other fixations never rise above our fixated worship of Yahweh. The Sabbath is also a gift from God…

It slows us down.

It makes us turn off.

It lets us listen.

It forces us to sit still…

And to know that He is God.

BACK TO JONAH

Fixation on God is important. It is the first point of triangulation when discerning God's will for your life. But fixation on God, in and of itself, is no guarantee of being in the center of God's perfect will. As we noted, Jonah was fixated on God, but he took off in the opposite direction of God's perfect will for him. That is why we need to look carefully at the other two questions, the other two points of triangulation, as they relate to God's perfect will for your life.

Q2: *What is your location?*

Chapter 4 –
Are We There Yet?

The plane touched down and my adrenaline was flowing. It was 10:00 p.m. local time, and dark. I could see little to nothing as I looked out the little porthole of a window on our Boeing 777, trying to get my first glimpse of Africa. I had never been this far from home before and I was wide-awake.

We deplaned down a set of stairs that had been pushed next to the exit of the plane; there are no jet-ways in this third world country of Tanzania. Our team of five made our way to the terminal, and then began the long process of filling out paperwork and moving through immigration and customs. A crisp, clean American $100 bill is all that is required to purchase a VISA. Things operate differently on the other side of the world.

Over an hour later, we made it out of the airport with our luggage, to be met by our host missionary Scott Ward. Only then was I able to get my first look at African terrain. Our final destination, the small Tanzanian town of Same, was still two and half hours away. Scott chose wisely to drive us only 15 minutes to the Kiriwe Hotel for the night; the road we had to travel to Same was frequented at night by bandits, and unsafe after dark.

Once in the Kiriwe, a delicious dinner of chicken and Stoney Tanagwizi soda was brought to our room, and we feasted at midnight. It was only 4:00 o'clock in the afternoon on our tired body clocks that had been up for over 30 hours. After dinner and exhausted, I finally collapsed into a foam mattress bed under a mosquito net to close my eyes for the first time in almost two days.

The funny thing about international travel is that the extreme shift in time zones plus jet lag does strange things to your body clock. About 3:00 a.m., I woke up and was wide-eyed. I decided to just lay in bed and think. I was leading a mission team from our church on this trip to Tanzania to help Scott in his effort to reach the people of Tanzania with the gospel of Christ.

Scott Ward was serving on staff at Grand Avenue Baptist Church when I began as its pastor in 2006. At the time, he had started the process with the International Mission Board to go to Tanzania with his wife, Jennifer, and two boys, Luke and Brennan. Scott had led several volunteer trips to Tanzania in the previous few years, and had felt the call of God to go to Tanzania as a full-time missionary. Specifically, Scott felt God calling him to work with an unreached people group called the Pare. The Pare people live in the Pare Mountains, just south and east of Mount Kilimanjaro, the highest mountain on the African continent. This was hard, cutting edge, ends-of-the-earth kind of mission work.

Once Scott was settled on the field, we began to provide state-side support via prayer, in addition to serving as his number-one church connection. The strategy that Scott had developed to reach the Pare called for volunteer teams from the United States to travel to Tanzania for 8-10 days at a time. The goal of each team was the establishment of a new church in one of the many villages of the Pare Mountains. I knew from the beginning that our church would be involved in sending at least a few of these teams. But as I prayed and communicated with Scott, I began to feel the distinct pull from the Holy Spirit that I needed to lead a trip myself.

As the lead pastor of a large church, I have to choose very carefully the various events and activities that occupy my time. There is only one of me and a seemingly endless variety of opportunities for ministry at any given time. I just cannot say "Yes" to everything. I have always had a love and appreciation for missions, having led two previous trips to England and one to Argentina. Our church also has a strong missions connection in Ecuador, working with another unreached people group called the Shuar. We send teams to Ecuador from our church each year, and while I have had a strong desire to go on one of those trips as well, the timing has never quite worked with my other travel obligations.

I felt that a trip to Tanzania was different. It was more than a "want" in terms of going, it was a "need to go" kind of feeling. The truth is, I didn't really *want* to go at all. Let me be transparent with you for a few minutes. You see, I hate to fly. I mean I really hate to fly. The truth is I'm a chicken. Yes, I admit it. You probably hear of people who have various fears or phobias. Well, I have a fear of flying. Part of this fear is that I just don't like not being in control. It's hard for me to sit there in a tightly confined space with little to no visibility, and put my life in the hands of a small group of people I have never met. The other part is just the plain old fear of crashing. Basically, I would rather drive for ten hours than fly for two to get to where I need to go.

But you can't drive to Africa. In fact, you can't drive to any of the places to which I have traveled for international mission trips. So I have learned to cope. I can either succumb to my fear and miss what God would have for me, or I can obey by going, and trust God to take care of me. I found a little trick to help me cope with the fear of crashing. In reading the reports of most plane crashes, it seems the majority of them occur either during take-off or shortly thereafter, usually within the first few minutes. The reports usually note something along the lines of, "Ninety seconds into flight such and such," or "Immediately after lift-off, flight so-and-so began to experience…." In fact, I don't think I've ever heard of a plane just crashing one hour into a long flight. So what I do is set a timer on my watch for five minutes. Once we take off and the timer hits five minutes, I start to relax. Okay, I know it sounds silly, but it works for me. And I'll bet some of you reading this know exactly what I'm talking about!

And so I found myself that night (or actually early in the morning), lying in a bed half way around the world, wide awake, and thinking that I was exactly where God wanted me to be. The key word in that last statement is the word *where*.

WHERE IN THE WORLD ARE YOU?

The word *where* is a word that denotes location. The second question that you need to answer as it relates to God's perfect will for your life is: *What is my location?* What we are talking about is geography. *Where* you are, literally, is critical to being able to discern God's will for your life.

Why would I take the time and energy to travel to Africa? Why would I muster up the courage to conquer a personal fear of flying and put myself on planes for a one hour, then a nine hour, and then another eight hour flight? And that's just one way; I still had to come home! Why would I do this? Why go to all the trouble and time and expense and fear? Because I had triangulated God's will for my life and knew that my geography required me to be in Africa leading that mission team. If I had gotten my geography wrong, I would have missed God's will and God's blessing.

Do you remember what we are told about Jonah's encounter with God? About God's revealed will for Jonah?

Jonah 1:1–2

Now the word of the LORD came to Jonah the son of Amittai, saying, "Arise, go to Nineveh, that great city, and call out against it, for their evil has come up before me."

God's will for Jonah involved a specific geographic location. Let me point out that although the book of Jonah does not tell us specifically where Jonah was when God came to him, we know from 2 Kings that Jonah's hometown was Gath-Hepher. It is a virtual certainty that this is where Jonah was when "the word of the LORD came" to him. That is important too.

Where should Jonah have been? Gath-Hepher, his hometown. Where was Jonah supposed to go? Ninevah, a pagan city. We know Jonah was where he was supposed to be or else God would not have come to him with such an important vocation. Had Jonah been somewhere else, very likely he would have lost his fixation and he might have gotten himself into trouble doing something he should not having been doing.

In fact, that is exactly what happened next and it all began with geography. Jonah was supposed to head to Nineveh. Nineveh was the only place that Jonah could be where God would continue to bless him. What Jonah should have done was follow the normal trade routes north through Damascus out of Israel and up into western Assyria, about 300-350 miles. Then he should have turned and headed directly east another 350-400 miles into the city of Nineveh. That's what Jonah *should* have done.

But what did Jonah actually do? He headed in exactly the opposite direction. You see, knowing the will of God and doing the will of God are two very different things. Jonah knew where he should be and what he *should* be doing. He chose, instead, to run.

MARY'S GEOGRAPHY

Mary emailed me and asked for an appointment. "Just need to talk," she said. As a rule, I never meet with a woman in my office alone, so we made arrangements to get together one afternoon with my assistant sitting in with us.

Mary's story is not uncommon. She has never really grown up in church, but came to know Christ a couple of years earlier and got really plugged in at Grand. She had a tough life before coming to Christ, and had a lot of friends who pulled her in directions that were not healthy. As happens with so many of us, Mary got busy. She's a wife and a mom of a beautiful little girl and she has a job. She's busy! And when people get too busy, things begin to slide and priorities begin to reshuffle. Church is often a casualty.

Eventually Mary hit rock bottom. Life got even tougher. She and her husband started arguing more. Mary began to hang out with friends who were not the best influence on her. Next she began to feel distant from God. She eventually found herself sitting in my office, spilling her guts to me. Her words to me were exactly this, "What is conviction? Because I think I have it." As Mary's life began to spin out of control, she did what many Christians naturally do: she shifted her fixation back to God. But fixation was not enough, because her geography was all wrong. "I know I need to get back in church, but I just don't know how," was her plea to me that day. I have heard this so many times. It is a simple issue of geography. And when I say simple, I mean simple. Yet we tend to make it so hard.

I think what Mary was really saying was that she had been away from church for so long that she did not know how to come back without feeling embarrassed. I looked at Mary, and as firmly and lovingly as I knew how, I told her, "Mary, just come. Get out of bed on Sunday and come. Period." I assured her that nobody was going to think ill of her, in fact everyone in her Bible study class would be excited to see her. She even admitted that they had been regularly contacting her and her husband, inviting them to various class socials and other events. Mary had just gotten her geography wrong.

When Mary's geography got messed up, so did her fixation. Or maybe it was the other way around. Actually, the two work hand-in-hand and I think you can see that. Where should Mary be on a Sunday morning? With her church family, worshipping God, laughing, studying her Bible, fixating on God. Where was she instead? Home, sleeping in, thinking about the night before or the week ahead, or thinking that she should be somewhere else, like church, and feeling guilty about it. It all comes down to geography.

JONAH'S BIG MISTAKE

Jonah got his geography all wrong too. I can understand not wanting to go to Nineveh. Seven hundred plus miles is a long way to travel by the standards of any day. It would have been expensive as well. Plus, these were people that Jonah just didn't want to be around, much less try to help. But Jonah didn't just ignore God's perfect will, he ran. Instead of heading northeast, he headed southwest, the exact opposite direction! Money must not have been the issue for Jonah either because his first stop was the seaport city of Joppa where he paid a fair to hitch a ride on a boat. Look at how the Bible explains Jonah's actions:

Jonah 1:3
But Jonah rose to flee to Tarshish from the presence of the LORD. He went down to Joppa and found a ship going to Tarshish. So he paid the fare and went on board, to go with them to Tarshish, away from the presence of the LORD.

We know where Nineveh is, but where is Tarshish? Scholars debate this, but it is likely that Tarshish refers to the most "distant" lands that people of that day would travel to from the Mediterranean Coast of Joppa. The most distant of these would have been have been the Phoenician colony of Tartessus, which is located on the southwestern coast of Spain. That's right, Spain! Approximately 2,200 miles from Joppa, and three times further away than Nineveh.

In all of this we can see Jonah's big mistake. He believed he could outrun God. Jonah may have had a proper fixation on God in order to receive prophetic words, but Jonah had a warped theology of God.

God is not bound by space and time as you and I are. In fact, God is the creator of space and time, and thus outside of space and time altogether. For Jonah to think that there was a place that he could run to where God was not, is foolishness to the point that I wonder if he really believed it was possible, in spite of his actions.

Don't we see people doing this all the time today? Even Christians who claim to believe in and worship God? I frequently see people making decisions in their lives as if God doesn't know or can't see. I've even done this. I'm sure you have too. This is self-deception. God's nature is such that He sees all and knows all. So when it comes to geography, God knows no bounds. We theologians have a word to describe this aspect of God's nature: we say He is *omnipresent*.

God is able to be anywhere and everywhere *at the same time*. This is mind boggling if you think about it. I can only be in one place at one time. That is why geography is so important. If God has ordained Plan A for my life, then this plan includes, by necessity, me being in the right location at the right time. As I asked in a previous chapter, what would have happened in my life had I not attended Oklahoma Baptist University, had I not made a geographic decision to speak at a high school retreat that my future wife had invited me to? What would have happened to Plan A for my life? And what about my wife? What would have happened to Plan A for her life had she been where she was supposed to be geographically, but I had missed my divine appointment to meet her there?

THE BUTTERFLY EFFECT

As I think back on my life, I marvel at the innumerable twists and turns it has taken. No decision in life stands on its own. Each choice is predicated on the choices that came before, and is itself the precursor of every choice that will follow.

Your life is the same way. Where are you right now? Literally, where are you? What is your location while you read this book? What decisions did you make in life today that paved the way to your current location, holding this book in your hands? Because you are where you are right now, that means you *aren't* somewhere else, maybe somewhere you should not be.

The point is this: we all make thousands of decisions on a daily basis. Where we will go. The route we will take to get there. When we leave and how fast we travel. And what we will do once we arrive. Every small detail of your life's journey on any given day orients the map of your life for what comes next. Statisticians call this the Butterfly Effect. The wind can blow in China, which leads to a chain of events that eventually cause a hurricane in the Gulf of Mexico. No decision in life stands alone.

We are all tempted at various points in life to go to certain places we know we should not go. I remember sneaking into a rated R movie when I was 15. It was the teen classic *The Breakfast Club*. I should not have been there. It's not that the movie warped me for life or anything like that, but it did cause me to lie to my parents about what movie I saw that night. In short, nothing good came from that experience.

When I was 17, my folks moved from our home in Fort Smith, Arkansas to Salt Lake City, Utah, because my dad was transferred. I had made friends the previous year with a girl in our youth group who was very needy. We used to talk on the phone and she used to tell me all her problems. At one point, I developed a crush on her and inquired if she wanted to be more than friends. She said, "No." Sure, my ego was hurt, but in retrospect this was the best thing.

I will never forget the week before our family actually made the move to Utah. This girl called me up and told me to meet her at a local hotel in town. She told me she wanted to have sex before I moved, and she said she'd pay for the hotel room. I was caught completely off guard by her proposal! But man, what a deal, huh? Every teenage boy's dream. The opportunity to experience sex and then be able to run off to another state and never have to face the consequences. This was a simple issue of geography. I did *not* need to go anywhere near that hotel. I needed to stay right where I was - at home, packing my belongings. I told my friend, "No." I told her it was wrong and nothing good could come of it. That was the last we ever spoke.

I am glad I was able to keep my location where it needed to be. What would have happened had I gotten my geography wrong that night? Maybe she would have gotten pregnant or maybe I would have contracted an STD, who knows. I am certain that no matter what would have happened in that hotel room that night, it would not have ended there. But Plan A might have ended. I might never have gone to OBU, and may have missed my divine appointment with Julie Dickson. That one decision of geography would have impacted my life, the life of my friend, my parents, and the life of my wife, Julie. Then when you consider that the three wonderful kids God has given me would not even exist, the consequences of geography suddenly become staggering.

Sex, Lies, and Geography

We see a similar story of bad geography played out in the life of King David. 2 Samuel 11 tells the fateful story of David and Bathsheba. Perhaps you know the tale. King David is on the roof of the palace late one afternoon, spending some time alone. As he is walking back and forth, his eye catches the naked body of Bathsheba bathing on a lower roofed home just down from David's view.

David sends for Bathsheba, he sleeps with her, and finds out later that he has impregnated her. In an effort to get out of trouble, he sends for Bathsheba's husband, Uriah, who is fighting a war on behalf of David. His hope is that Uriah will sleep with Bathsheba upon returning home and thus explain the pregnancy. But Uriah does not cooperate. He feels duty-bound while back in Jerusalem to restrain himself from life's pleasures while his fellow soldiers are in battle. Enraged, David sends Uriah back to the war with orders to place him on the front lines, hoping he will be killed in battle, which he is. This frees David to marry Bathsheba and thus save the embarrassment of a bastard child.

How could such a mess happen in the first place? It's all about geography. A good question to ask would be, why was David on that roof in the first place? As king he should have been at war with his troops. David's geography was all wrong. Next, he ordered Bathsheba to place herself in a bad geographic zone, David's bed. Then he placed Uriah in two ill-conceived geographic zones, first Jerusalem, away from the battle, and then the very front line of battle where he would eventually be killed.

David's poor choice of geography and location led to a series of bad events, not only for himself, but also for the innocent people around him. You see, geography and location are so important. Not just for your life, but for the lives of those around you.

Chapter 5 –
The Domino Effect

Jonah thought he could run from God.

Jonah thought that his own sinful actions would only affect him.

Jonah was wrong on both counts.

No matter where you go, God is there. As you attempt to run from God, you will find that you are only running into Him time after time. In the midst of running into God, you will discover that He is pursuing you. If you are a believer in Christ running from God, know this – God will hunt you down. You have been bought with a price. You belong to Him. He will not let you get away. And He was not about to let Jonah get away.

There is also a Domino Effect when it comes to running from God's will. If you are not geographically where you need to be at a given time, that means you are somewhere else that you should not be. Because nobody lives in a vacuum, the people in your life and the people who cross your path while you are mis-located are all of a sudden at risk. The idea that we are only at risk of hurting ourselves when we defy God's will is a lie.

In the last chapter, we saw in the book of Jonah how Jonah had jumped a ship to Tarshish in an attempt to flee "the presence of the LORD." Let's look at what happened next:

Jonah 1:4–5
But the LORD hurled a great wind upon the sea, and there was a mighty tempest on the sea, so that the ship threatened to break up. Then the mariners were afraid, and each cried out to his god. And they hurled the cargo that was in the ship into the sea to lighten it for them. But Jonah had gone down into the inner part of the ship and had lain down and was fast asleep.

Verse four is a clear picture of the holy hunt that God is on as He seeks to get Jonah back on track. Notice that every other person on the ship is at risk. Now these are clearly not Christian men. We see that they each are praying to their own god as the ship is being tossed about. The men are scared to death. They truly believe that they are about to die. I believe that God would have taken that ship to the bottom of the ocean if that is what it was going to take to get Jonah back.

Let me ask you a question at this point - why are these men at risk, at the point of death at sea? Is it because they are pagans and don't worship Yahweh? Is it because of some sin they have committed as a crew, or because of some evil the captain has done? The answer is NO. They are standing on the brink of death because Jonah is in the wrong geographic location. It's as simple as that. That is the thing about sin, it always has a Domino Effect. The smallest of sins in our minds always creates a tidal wave that can devastate those closest to us.

Let's put the Jonah narrative in a modern context. What if your church was offering the opportunity for an international mission trip to a country like Tanzania, targeting an unreached people group like the Pare? What if you sensed the distinct and unmistakable call of God to go on this trip? But what if you did not want to pay the price? What if when your pastor came to you and asked you to go, you lied and told him you had other plans, say vacation plans? What if you actually made other travel plans to "cover" yourself so that you'd have an excuse not to go on the mission trip? What if?

Jump ahead to travel day. While the mission team is headed overseas in one plane, you and your family are in another plane headed to the ski slopes. What would be your reaction if I told you that God was not going to put up with your disobedience? What if I told you that you were putting every living soul on that plane, including your own family, at risk of death all because *your* geography was wrong? "Preposterous" you say. Really? Is it really so crazy to think that God would pursue you? That your disobedience to God's perfect will would endanger innocent lives? Just look at Jonah. Isn't that exactly what was happening to the people on that boat?

The truth is, most of us never think this way when we make decisions about what we want to do or not do; or when we make decisions about whether or not we are going to let God dictate our geographic path through life. We tend to zone out and live our lives as if we are the only ones impacted by our decisions. Jonah teaches us something completely different.

Zoned Out

It's really no surprise that we have this problem with zoning out to the Domino Effect of our geographic choices. Jonah was zoned out as well. Isn't that what the text indicates in verse five? We are told that while everyone was topside during this raging storm, fearing for their lives and praying to their gods, Jonah was in the hull fast asleep.

You may read that and be thinking, "Man, how clueless can Jonah be?" That's understandable, I mean, how do you sleep through a storm that is tossing everyone else around? I've already confessed my fear of flying. Let me confess something else. Whenever I do fly and the plane runs into turbulence, I get really frustrated with people who just sleep right through it. You know who I'm talking about. You've seen them too. The plane is being rocked up and down and all over the sky. The "fasten seat belt" sign comes on. Cabin service is discontinued and the flight attendant comes on the intercom to tell everyone to return to their seats. I've been on planes where the turbulence is so bad that I physically begin to feel ill. My palms are sweating and my nails are digging into the armrests. But then there is always that one guy, usually sitting next to me, just snoozing away. My flesh wants to reach out and slap him and yell, "Come on, man! Wake up! We're all about to die here!" But I don't. At least I haven't yet. But you get the idea. Some people just zone out in the midst of disaster.

Okay, I'll admit that what's disaster to one man might just be a routine flight with air turbulence to another. It is true to say, however, that in the midst of real disaster, some people just don't get it. Remember that as the Titanic was sinking, the band continued to play and gym instructors continued to work with passengers.

Jonah was on the Titanic. I have no doubt that boat was going down, and he was the only one who was checked out. How is this possible? Because this is what sin does. It desensitizes us to the disaster looming all around; even when the disaster is obvious to everyone else.

PRESTON'S PANTIES

One of the saddest times in my ministry involved a family in our church. Preston and Sue were the perfect picture of a model Christian home, at least on the outside. Preston was a gifted musician who played bongos in our church band and sang solos from time-to-time. Sue was a saint of a Christian young lady with a gentle and sweet spirit. Together they had a beautiful son they were rearing in the church. Preston had a good job and Sue ran a wonderful home for the whole family. All was bliss...until Sue called me one New Year's Eve. Preston was leaving her and his son for another woman.

Preston, as it turned out, had a problem with Internet pornography. In addition, he had become consumed with Internet chat rooms and had met a woman much younger than Sue who lived in another state. The truth began to come out, as it always does. We learned that as Preston would make out-of-town business trips, he would make arrangements to rendezvous with this other woman. They began a sexual relationship and they began to make plans. Her plan was to leave the man who was the father of her baby boy (to whom she was not married), and move to Fort Smith to begin a new life with Preston. Preston's plan was to leave his family and start over with this new family.

They both pulled the trigger on their plans and set up their new home in town in an apartment complex. Sue was as devastated as any wife and mother I have ever seen. Family and close friends made numerous attempts to call Preston to repentance. But Preston's sin had completely desensitized him to the utter destruction in the lives of the innocent people all around him.

Our church was impacted. They were a high profile couple. People who knew them best were just shaking their heads asking how this could happen. Couples in their Bible study class came to the aid of Sue to cry with and pray for her. Preston's parents in another city in Arkansas were crushed, and the news soon spread to their church as well. Preston had extended family in our church that were hurt and angered by his actions. It seemed that everywhere I went, I could see the "ship going down." The only one who could not see it was Preston. It seemed like he was asleep in the hull.

I will never forget confronting Preston in his apartment. I was there to plead with him to repent and return to his first loves – Jesus and Sue. I found myself sitting in the living room of a one bedroom apartment. The place was a pit. There was little to no furniture, food boxes on the floor, and a tiny TV in the corner. Preston's girlfriend and her baby had retreated to the bedroom upon my arrival. Preston and I sat across from each other as I tried to make him see all that he was giving up. He had walked way from a nice house to live in that mess. He had walked away from a virtuous woman to live with a woman that we all knew would leave him in a matter of months. There was nothing there that would last. I asked Preston if he was prepared to lose it all, to see his wife marry another man, and to see his son call that man Dad. He said he was. But I'll never forget the look of "deadness" that covered Preston's face. I could tell he was totally checked out. In fact, the whole time we talked about coming back to his family, he was occupying himself with folding a basket of laundry. At one point he even pulled out his girlfriend's panties and folded them in front of me! That, my friend, is what sin does. It desensitizes you to the point where a man can fold the panties of his mistress while being rebuked by his pastor.

Preston's geography was all out of whack. He should never have been sitting in that chair at that computer looking at pictures of naked women and talking to other women in chat rooms. He should never have met that woman in that hotel while on an out-of-state business trip. He should not have moved out of his house and moved into that apartment. In so many ways, time after time, the very simple issue of geography played into the scheme of things.

There is no doubt that Preston had abandoned God's Plan A for his life. Now his wife and son would have to pay the price as well. The Domino Effect. It could have all been so easily avoided. You see, knowing God's perfect will for your life isn't as complicated as we make it. If Preston had just paused and asked a couple of simple questions, things might have been different. What is my fixation? What is my location? What *should* I be fixated on? Where *should* I be located?

So simple, yet so simple to miss as well.

Keep It Simple

It's so simple that even pagans get it. Let's jump back to our story of Jonah. Jonah is desensitized. He's checked out. People are about to die because he's in the wrong location and he doesn't have a clue. The pagan sailors on the ship, however, understand that something needs to be done. They also understand the concept of fixation. Let's look again at the text:

Jonah 1:6
So the captain came and said to him, "What do you mean, you sleeper? Arise, call out to your god! Perhaps the god will give a thought to us, that we may not perish."

Here we have a pagan captain of a merchant boat who understands that the supernatural is greater than the natural. He knows that when we come to the end of ourselves, we need help. He understands the concept of prayer. It's amazing

63

if you think about it. Jonah is a prophet of the one true and living God. He has a direct link to the Creator. He is the key to the whole thing. Yet he is the one standing in the way. While at the very same time, a bunch of godless men are crying out to their gods in a desperate act of humility. The pagan is instructing the Christian in the ways of God.

But Jonah is stubborn. There is no indication in the text that Jonah prayed to God. Remember, what he is trying to do is run from God. And because he is focused on running, he misses the very simple act of prayer. I wonder as I look at the text what would have happened if Jonah had fallen on his knees in an act of contrition and cried out to God for forgiveness. Would the storm have ceased right then and there? If Jonah had submitted to God's will and promised to go to Nineveh, would the events that were to follow have been avoided? By re-fixating on God and promising to get his geography in order, Jonah might have saved himself a whole lot of grief, and the sailors their cargo. But Jonah could not master the simple.

What about you? Are you missing the simple things in your walk with Christ? The very easy things that you know you need to be about doing, but you just fail to do? How often do you pray? What about reading your Bible? These are fixation things. Do you have a church? How often do you attend? How often do you find "other" things to keep you from worshipping with the family of God? Vacation, travel ball, long weekends, college football trips. It adds up really quick and before you know it, you feel distant from God and your friends and it really is nothing more than a simple issue of geography.

Don't make finding the will of God hard.

Keep it simple.

THE GOD OF CHANCE

I introduced you in chapter three to Gad, the god of chance. Millions of people today place their future in the hands of Gad. They may not worship him as Gad by name, or bow to an idolic image, but the worship of the god of chance is alive and well. It has been this way since the beginning of time.

The sailors on Jonah's ship were in a state of desperation. A massive storm was swamping the boat. They had already tossed the cargo, losing any opportunity for profit. They had turned to their pagan gods in prayer. Now, as a last shot, they turn to chance. Perhaps they can discover *who* has brought this calamity on them, and in so doing find a way of escape. With Jonah finally awake and joined with the rest of the men on the deck of the boat, they cast lots.

Jonah 1:7–8

And they said to one another, "Come, let us cast lots, that we may know on whose account this evil has come upon us." So they cast lots, and the lot fell on Jonah. Then they said to him, "Tell us on whose account this evil has come upon us. What is your occupation? And where do you come from? What is your country? And of what people are you?"

What do you think? Is it a mere coincidence that the lot fell on Jonah? Of course not. What we see here is the clear hand of God at work. Remember, God is pursuing Jonah…and God can do anything He wants to do. If He can manipulate the weather and call a storm to sink a boat, how hard would it really be for God to turn a die or cause a lot to fall in Jonah's direction?

Let me be clear in what I am saying and not saying. I am not saying that God is an advocate of reliance on chance. I am not saying that you should go out today and buy a lottery ticket because God will cause the local Power Ball to fall in your favor. I am not saying that you should run over to the local casino this evening and play a hand of Blackjack, or pull the lever on the slots because God works in this way. That is not what I am saying.

What I am saying is this: God controls everything. In God's economy there is not such a thing as chance. God can and will do what He has to do to get your attention and push you toward His Plan A for your life. He may bend weather if that is what it takes. He may orchestrate an email from a friend at just the right time to send you a message. He may cause you to literally stumble and fall down and sprain an ankle, if that is what He must do to get you back on track.

What we don't know from reading the story of Jonah is all that God had already done to get Jonah's attention. Things that Jonah had ignored. I am confident there were many checks that God placed in the path of Jonah as he ran first to Joppa, then found the right boat headed in the wrong direction. Who knows what Jonah had to do to acquire the finances for the voyage, and the various ways God may have tried to prevent him from going in the wrong direction. I believe that God works on us gently at first, only moving to more extreme measures as our own stubbornness moves us away from Plan A.

Please read and remember this next phrase: *never* underestimate what God will do to get your attention.

A Question of Geography

Once the lot lands on Jonah the jig is up. These salty sailors are convinced that Jonah is the key to their calamity. Now come the questions to Jonah. Notice what they ask him. "Where do you come from? What is your country? And of what people are you?" Just look at those three questions.

They all deal with geography! These pagan men got it. They had a keen sense that Jonah was out of place. They wanted to know *where* he had come from. Maybe that would explain why he was there, with them, incurring the wrath of God.

Let's look at Jonah's response to their questioning:

Jonah 1:9–10
And he said to them, "I am a Hebrew, and I fear the LORD, the God of heaven, who made the sea and the dry land." Then the men were exceedingly afraid and said to him, "What is this that you have done!" For the men knew that he was fleeing from the presence of the LORD, because he had told them.

Jonah doesn't pull any punches. He fesses up to who he is and where he is from. This is the first clue that Jonah has come to his senses, that he is beginning to understand the Domino Effect of consequences that his misplaced geography has caused. In fact, these are the first words uttered by Jonah in the whole book. By identifying himself as a Hebrew, he is making a statement about what land he is from and Who he worships. Jonah is even more specific, "I fear the LORD." Some versions of the English Bible provide the alternate translation of this phrase, "I worship Yahweh." This is a statement of fixation, and as I have said, fixation is all about worship.

That was all the men of the ship needed to hear. They had great respect for the Hebrew God and because Jonah had apparently told these men previously that he was running from God, they now knew that he was the source of their crisis.

This admission in verse ten gives us another insight into Jonah's psyche. Not only was Jonah running from Plan A for his life, but he knew it and was even willing to verbally testify to it. It reminds me so much of Preston, who looked me in the eye as I was confronting him about his affair, when he said that he knew what he was doing was wrong but he just didn't care. That was Jonah. He knew he was running from God and he didn't care. He didn't even mind telling others about it. You almost get the notion that he was bragging about it. Jonah knew what Plan A was for his life, he just didn't agree with Plan A. He had opted instead for Plan B.

We don't ever find out what Jonah's Plan B was beyond escape to Tarshish. Was he planning to stay there the rest of his life? Did he have a trade in mind? Or was he just flying by the seat of his pants? We will never know. But what we do know is that he was willfully fleeing Plan A. When I am asked by people about finding God's will for their lives, I wonder many times if they don't know full well what God would have for them, they just don't like it and are looking for a viable alternative that God would bless. There is more of Jonah in all of us than we would ever want to admit, I think.

TOM'S TEMPEST

Tom was a Jonah. Tom was a great guy, he just had a problem with his geography. Tom, it seemed, was constantly finding himself in the wrong place. And not just at the wrong times. The places Tom would find himself are places where there never is a good time.

Tom had already endured one divorce due to his infidelity. He had then begun to make good decisions. He fixated on God, became very active in church, and was blessed with a wonderful woman as his wife. But Tom lost all control of his geography. Very late one night while his wife was out of town, he decided to drive across state lines to the "local" casino. That was his first mistake. Where should Tom have been? Home. Where was he? A casino.

Casinos tend to draw other less savory businesses around them. An adult establishment had set up shop next door to the casino where Tom was. On his way home he decided to stop at the adult store. Another bad geographic decision. That very night, this adult store was the target of a police sting for men seeking to proposition women. Yeah, you guessed it. Tom got caught up in the sting. He insisted that he was set up, and maybe he was. But it was really all about geography, wasn't it?

Shortly after the casino / adult store night, Tom had another setback. While out on a sales call one afternoon, he made the poor decision to stop at a local park. This particular park in our city has a bad reputation for being a place where a lot of homosexual activity and prostitution takes place. Tom insisted that he had to stop to go to the restroom. He *really* had to go, he explained. But you've probably guessed what happened next. Yes, another police sting. And another set up, Tom claimed. And it is very possible that all of this was a big misunderstanding. But the point, once again, is geography. I make no bones about it. I have told every man in my church to never, under any circumstances, go to this particular park. No good can come of it.

Tom would end up divorced for a second time and embroiled in legal trouble because of the two sting operations. As I said, he really is a good guy, and last I heard he had begun to make good decisions again and had been keeping his geography in order. That's one more important thing to note about this whole geography thing. It is easy to change. If you are not where you are supposed to be, just leave. Immediately. Get in the car and go! Wherever you know you need to be, get there. Don't wait. Make the move now.

And that's exactly what Jonah did next.

JONAH'S JUMP

The sailors knew Jonah held the answer. They wanted to know from him how to make all of this stop. Look at the exchange:

Jonah 1:11–13

Then they said to him, "What shall we do to you, that the sea may quiet down for us?" For the sea grew more and more tempestuous. He said to them, "Pick me up and hurl me into the sea; then the sea will quiet down for you, for I know it is because of me that this great tempest has come upon you." Nevertheless, the men rowed hard to get back to dry land, but they could not, for the sea grew more and more tempestuous against them.

The storm is growing ever worse. Death is certain. I do not believe that this was some mere exercise in obedience that God was walking Jonah through. I do not believe that this was some display of God's power in order to convert these pagan men to become worshipers of the one true and living God. I believe that this was an act of finality. God was going to use this storm to kill everyone on board that ship if that is what it took to assert His rightful control over Jonah's life.

You see, that is really what this whole conversation of God's will is all about. Control. Who is really in control? God or you? God is the one that created you. He is the one that breathed life into you. You belong to Him. Once you become a Christian, you have bought into God's system. He has a very specific role for you to play. As I have said, God's desire is for your life to be one of immense blessing (for you and through you to others), all in preparation for heaven. But you must give the map to God. He has to be the one that navigates. He will let you drive, but He is the one really in control. Without a map, you are just out for a drive heading who knows where. Which is exactly the position that most of humanity is in. But God has given us some very simple tools, the very three questions we are asking in this book, to help us find our position on His map.

Jonah was ready to get back on track. Actually, I believe that Jonah felt that Plan A for his life was lost. I think he knew he'd blown it. He never dreamed that his actions would lead to the deaths of innocent men. But facing reality, Jonah was not willing to be the cause of their demise. If anyone was to die, it should be him and him alone.

Jonah was ready to take his medicine. He believed that a simple adjustment in geography would end the storm and save the lives of the crew. "Throw me overboard," was Jonah's solution. Is Jonah ready to jump? I don't necessarily think so or else he would have just done it. Think about it. It's one thing to know you need to go overboard, but another thing to take the plunge unassisted. Jonah isn't that strong. But he is strong enough to let them throw him over the side of the ship. He won't fight.

The doomed crew, however, just can't bring themselves to do it. You have to admire them for this. Whereas Jonah fails to measure the cost of his actions, a cost that would end up including the lives of these men, the crew is unwilling to pay the price of Jonah's life to calm the storm. These men are heroic in their actions. They determine to try and row through the storm and save all of their lives.

It is all for naught. The storm, or rather God, is too strong. In the end, there is only one thing left to do, only one thing that can be done. And so they pick Jonah up and over the side he goes, "and the sea ceased from its raging."

It's amazing what the simple geographic move of just a few feet can do to stop the dominos from falling.

Q3: *What is your vocation?*

CHAPTER 6 –
CHRISTIANITY BEYOND CONVERSION

I became a Christian in 1984. I remember the moment with crystal clarity, as if it was yesterday. I accepted Christ as my Lord and Savior on the last day of a Rick Stanley youth revival my church was hosting. I can still recall the emotions and feelings in the days and hours leading up to my surrender. I was wrenched inside. I knew God was calling me to Himself but I was resisting. When I finally gave in and gave up it was like taking the top off of a Coke bottle you've been shaking. I remember feeling relief and feeling free. It was an amazing moment.

That is why I was confused when the same sense of "pressure" began building inside of me once again in the months following my conversion. What did this mean? Did I miss some step or do something wrong? Why was I starting to get that feeling that God wanted me to do something else? It was like the Coke bottle was starting to shake again and the pressure build.

As a new Christian, I made the same mistake that many new Christians make - thinking that conversion is the beginning and end of God's work in my life. Conversion is certainly the beginning, but it is by no means the end. This is why the apostle Paul exhorts us in his letter to the Philippians to "work out your own salvation with fear and trembling" (Phil. 2:12). Salvation is a process that begins with conversion. Once I converted, I had taken the first step of many more to come.

ORDO SALUTIS

The Reformation brought to us a great expansion in theological thinking, as well as a return to orthodoxy based on *Sola Scriptura*, Scripture Alone. The Reformers also gave us the *Ordo Salutis*, the Order of Salvation. The term used by Lutherans in the early 1700s is conceptually drawn from the following passage of Paul's letter to the Romans.

Romans 8:29–30
For those whom he foreknew he also predestined to be conformed to the image of his Son, in order that he might be the firstborn among many brothers. And those whom he predestined he also called, and those whom he called he also justified, and those whom he justified he also glorified.

The *Ordo Salutis* is a sequential list of steps that a person walks through as he "works out (his) salvation." The most common terms in the *Ordo Salutis* are:

1. **Foreknowledge** – God knows those who will come to Him seeking salvation.

2. **Predestination** – Based on His foreknowledge, God puts in place a plan to bring individuals to a saving knowledge.

3. **Calling** – Jesus is proclaimed to the one predestined.

4. **Regeneration** – One is born again and receives new life via the Holy Spirit.

5. **Conversion** – The spirit enables faith and repentance on the part of the one regenerated.

6. **Justification** – The legal standing before God of the one converted is now: not guilty.

7. **Adoption** – into the family of God.

8. **Sanctification** – Life-long growth to be more like Jesus – discipleship.

9. **Perseverance** – The ongoing relationship with Jesus.

10. **Death** – The body is separated from the spirit.

11. **Glorification** – The spirit is reunited with a new body.[1]

Depending on the sources you study, you may discover the previous list in various forms with different terms. And depending on your theological tradition and bent, you may take exception with certain definitions. But the most important idea behind the *Ordo Salutis* is that salvation is a *process*. It is a process where God works and where you work.

I like the *Ordo Salutis*, and at the same time I don't like it. I like it from the standpoint that it illustrates clearly that my life is a process of walking toward God. I have not arrived yet. There is an arrogance that creeps into the church among those who have been Christians for most of their lives. It is an arrogance of *arrival*. It is an arrogance that says, "I've got it figured out. Just follow me and you won't go wrong." It is an arrogance that forces personal preferences and not sound theology onto others, usually those who are brand-new to the faith. It is an arrogance that runs people away from the church and ultimately dooms a church to decline and eventual death. *Ordo Salutis* reminds me, reminds all of us, that none of us are there yet. We *all* have a *long* way to go.

On the other hand, I don't like the *Ordo Salutis* because it smacks of cookie cutter-ism. On the surface it looks like a mold that all Christians just stand in line to pour themselves into. But the fact is, there is great diversity in the body of Christ. Everyone has a unique story of how they came to Christ. No two stories are exactly the same. That means that the story of Christian growth will be equally as unique.

I have stated in the outset of this book that God has a unique plan for your life, Plan A. Plan A for me is not going to look like Plan A for you. We are different, and the beauty of our God is that He revels in our diversity. He loves to create and He is a highly creative God. What is the imagery of creativity? Uniqueness. If I were able to paint an exact replica of Van Gogh's *Sunflowers*, you would not say that I was creative, you would say that I was just a copy-cat. God doesn't make copies, He paints unique portraits on the canvas of each and every life. But we don't see this in the *Ordo Salutis*. We need something more.

From the perspective of God's will for your life, I would say that God takes the *Ordo Salutis* and customizes it for each person in the world. This is what it means to "work out" *your* salvation.

A WORK IN PROGRESS

Let me jump back now to this growing sense of unease I was experiencing in the months that followed my conversion to Christianity. In retrospect, I know now that what was happening was God working out His Plan A for my life. At a certain point, I can't even remember when, the thought struck me that perhaps God was calling me into vocational ministry. At the age of 14, I had no idea what that really meant. So I went looking for help.

I set up meetings with my youth minister, J.B. Collingsworth, and my pastor, Dr. James W. Bryant. Both men were gracious to take time to speak with me. "How do you know if God is calling you into the ministry?" was my question to these men. They both answered in similar fashion. They both told me to take it slow and *be sure* that God was calling me. J.B. told me to think about other things in my life that I might want to do and see if my heart's affection regarding vocation would move to something else. Dr. Bryant was more direct, "If you can stay out of the ministry, do it!" He then clarified, "Jeff, if you're not called to the ministry, you will never make it." Both men were telling me that the call of God had to be clear and certain. A decision to move into the ministry as a vocation had to be something that I was compelled to do by God, and not something that should be pursued because I thought it would be a great thing to do.

As time ticked away over the next few months, it became unmistakable and unavoidable that God was calling and I had to answer. So I did. And once again, the top was taken off the Coke bottle and the sense of relief returned. I have learned over the years to listen to that sense of unease. It usually means God is about to do something new in my life.

Even after I gave in, after I accepted my call to the ministry, I still did not know exactly what it was I would actually do in the ministry. For several years this would bother me. I would meet other guys going into the ministry, and they all seemed to know where they were headed, be it youth ministry, music, or the pastorate. When I made it to college at OBU they were everywhere - people who knew exactly what they were going to do. "I'm going to be a youth pastor." Or "I'm going to pastor a church." Most of my friends knew what direction in ministry they were headed...but not me. All I knew was that I was called and I was willing to do whatever God wanted me to do. It's clear to me now that this was all a part of Plan A for me. What I was seeing in the lives of others was Plan A for them. No two Plan As are the same. But the God that writes the Plan is.

You may not be a pastor, in fact, you probably aren't. You are probably just a regular person trying to figure out God's plan for your life. It doesn't matter that I am writing from the perspective of a pastor. Being a pastor is Plan A for me, but I promise you this, God has a Plan A for you as well. That Plan A will be played out and revealed as you walk the *Ordo Salutis* in your life.

I actually haven't always been a pastor. My pathway through vocational ministry has been a work in progress, much the same way that my whole life is a work in progress. I was a youth minister at the Morning Star Baptist Church in Meeker, Oklahoma while at OBU. After college, I worked on a church growth project in Baton Rouge, Louisiana for Parkview Baptist Church. My job was to help envision, strategize and implement a new alternative worship service for the church. Then I served the Comite Baptist Church in Baton Rouge working with singles and discipleship. My next stopping point was seminary in Fort Worth, Texas, but I also served a portion of my time there as the pastor of the Valley View Baptist Church, a small rural church in Spanish Fort, Texas. After seminary, Julie and I moved to Park City, Utah to plant a church that ultimately failed. We then ended up in Springdale, Arkansas for the next nine years where I served as Bible teacher, campus pastor, and later, secondary dean for Shiloh Christian School. Mixed in that time frame was ministry to college students and assisting the launch staff of a multi-site campus for First Baptist Church in the city of Rogers, Arkansas. All of this was my path before coming to pastor the Grand Avenue Baptist Church in Fort Smith, Arkansas where I currently serve as of the writing of this book.

It may look like I have been all over the map, and as I look at the last paragraph, it sure looks that way to me! But there are many, many stories and facets to the journey I laid out above that I just don't have the time to go into in these pages. I can tell you that each and every step was a stone that paved the way to the next. In hindsight, it was all a part of God's Plan A for me. Each and every move and change marked a crossroads, a point where I had to fall on my face and plead with God to show me the way. "Is it time to move? Or should we stay?" "Should we take this new ministry position? Should I go back to school?" My life's journey, in terms of my vocational ministry, represents prayer and tears as I seek God's perfect will and not just His permissive will. As Julie was added into the mix and then later three children, the stakes for each decision only grew.

That is ultimately why I am writing this book. Because no matter what Plan A is for your life, we all come to these major crossroads in our lives. As we walk up to the intersection, we have a distinct sense that we better get it right. What I am telling you is that getting it right doesn't have to be hard. It doesn't have to be feared. In fact, if you live your life according to the principle presented in this book, the principle of triangulation, I am telling you that when you arrive at the crossroads you will just know which way to go.

It's all about living your life, each and every day, in the little things, the no-brainers, asking and answering the three simple questions I am giving you:

1. What is my fixation?
2. What is my location?
3. What is my vocation?

We've already looked at the first two questions, and now we are looking at the third. In fact, the third question is what I have *already* been talking about this whole chapter: What is my vocation?

VOCATION IS MORE THAN A JOB

What do you want to be when you grow up? Isn't that the question we're all asked at some point while we are children? The question is one of vocation. What job do you want to have one day?

I wanted to be a lot of things when I was a kid: police officer, astronaut, a lawyer like Perry Mason, etc. I ended up being a pastor, or at least that is what I am right now. The end, hopefully, has not been reached, and God only knows what is next for Jeff Crawford.

We tend to equate our identities with our jobs. When you meet someone for the first time, after you ask them their name, what is the next thing you want to know about them? "What do you do for a living?" is the common question. What someone does, their vocation, becomes an identifier that shapes the way we view them as a whole. Right or wrong, that's just the way it is.

When I meet someone for the first time, like my child's new teacher for the school year, I try to keep it a secret for as long as possible that I am a pastor. Why? Because I know that the moment someone finds out I am a pastor they will immediately profile me, and I know that there is so much more to who I am beyond what someone thinks when they hear the word *pastor*.

I think it's this way with all of us. My dad was an over-the-road truck driver for 40 years before his retirement. So let me ask, what comes to your mind when you here the words *truck driver*? I can promise that whatever thoughts or images come into your mind, it isn't my dad. He broke the stereotype. When my dad left home, he always carried a hard-shell suitcase full of clean clothes. His jeans would be washed, ironed and starched with a crease down the middle. He would wear a button-up long sleeve shirt, also ironed and tucked in. His cowboy boots would be shined and spotless. That was my dad. No white t-shirt with a cigarette pack rolled into the sleeve. No greasy hair or dirt under the fingernails. No foul language on his tongue. None of it. My dad was a consummate professional. He did well in his profession and God blessed him. As a result, our whole family was blessed.

What about you?

What do you do?

What is your job?

Your vocation?

A better question to ask would be *who* are you? The answer to that question is definitely related to vocation, but your vocation is so much more than merely what you do to draw a paycheck. In its most literal sense, vocation is what you *do*. I mean what you do moment-by-moment, day-to-day.

Confused? Let me put it this way: what are doing right now? That's easy, you are reading! And that's what I am talking about. Your vocation right now is the act of reading this book. That tells me something about you. It tells me that you care about who you are and what God has for you by way of a plan. It tells me that you care about God and the things of God. It tells me something about your fixation. It also tells me something about your location. Oh, I may not know exactly where you are physically located right now, but I do know where you are not located. You're not in a casino, or a strip club, or, well, you get the idea. You are probably in a safe place, someplace that you actually belong. A place that's good for you.

I know all of this based on your vocation.

Yes, vocation is so much more than just a job.

JONAH'S JOB

Jonah was a prophet. That was his vocation. He was also probably a farmer of grapes. This is a good guess based on his village of Gath-Hepher being a place where wine was produced. So Jonah was actually bi-vocational. When the story of Jonah begins, we see that he is fixated on God. This is how "the word of the Lord" was able to come to him. We see him geographically located in his hometown. But we don't see Jonah *doing* anything. This prophet of God needs a vocation, he needs something to do. What do prophets do? They preach. But Jonah had nobody to preach to and no word to speak, so God sent him to preach with a specific message for a specific people.

By now you know how the story unfolds, but let me ask and answer some obvious questions:

What should Jonah be fixated on? God.

Where should Jonah be? Nineveh.

What should Jonah be doing? Preaching.

That's what Jonah *should* be all about. Had Jonah asked these three questions, had he triangulated his position, he would never have gotten himself and those around him into so much trouble. He would have remained on the track that we are calling Plan A. As I said, that's what Jonah should have been all about. Instead:

What was Jonah fixated on? Plan B.

Where was Jonah located? On a ship to Tarshish.

What was he doing? Running.

Jonah missed it on all three counts. I believe that for Jonah, it all began to go wrong over the issue of vocation. Jonah didn't want to do his job. He didn't want to do what he was supposed to do. This led to misplaced fixation and misplaced location. Once again, do you see how all of these points triangulate? How they all impact each other? How they can be used as a check-and-balance on each other and in your life? That is why asking these three questions in your own life can be powerful! *Before* you come to a major crossroads, live your life asking and answering these questions in the right way. Then when you arrive at the intersection, you will instinctively know which way to go - what God's perfect will is. It will seem almost natural, not veiled or mysterious at all.

WHAT ARE YOU DOING HERE?!

Jonah's issue wasn't one of not knowing which way to go or what to do. He knew exactly what God wanted him to do and where He wanted him to be. Jonah just chose to go in the other direction. He chose willfully to pursue Plan B.

We have already seen what the consequences are for those around us when we choose to willfully disobey God - The Domino Effect. Now let's go back to the storm that is threatening to sink the boat that Jonah is on, along with all the innocent lives. As the sailors are trying to figure out why this storm has come upon them, Jonah is revealed as the source. Look one more time at their reaction:

Jonah 1:8
Then they said to him, "Tell us on whose account this evil has come upon us. What is your occupation? And where do you come from? What is your country? And of what people are you?"

Do you see it?! It's right there in front of us. Look at the very first question these men asked Jonah, "What is your occupation?" In other words, what is your vocation? They knew that what Jonah was doing, or rather, what he should be doing, was directly related to the calamity that had befallen them.

Once they knew he was a prophet of God, they put it all together. He had already told them he was running from God. That part probably didn't faze them. I am sure there have been many a sailor who have run from God as well. They were probably used to transporting people all the time who were running from something or someone. But once they found out that he was a *prophet* who was running from God, that dramatically changed their perspective.

You can almost read between the lines. "You're a what?! A prophet! And you're running from God? Well, what are you doing here? Man, you should be in Nineveh!!" The Bible actually says it this way:

Jonah 1:10
Then the men were exceedingly afraid and said to him, "What is this that you have done!" For the men knew that he was fleeing from the presence of the LORD, because he had told them.

Look at the phrase they use - "What is this you have done!" This is a statement more than a question. It's a statement about vocation. "What have you *done.*" These seamen may not have been the kind to be in touch with God, but they knew enough about divinity to know that Jonah had blown it. He'd gotten his vocation all wrong. And they were the ones paying the price with him.

THINKING STRAIGHT ABOUT YOUR VOCATION
I want us to think straight when it comes to the issue of your vocation. So let me be clear - your vocation is not your job. It is not what you do for a living. It is not what you do to bring money home. All of these fit into your vocation, but they are not the total of your vocation.

Your vocation is very simply everything you *do*. Period. When you are traveling to the grocery store, you are *doing*. When you are pumping gas, you are *doing*. When you are studying for a test, you are *doing*. When you are drinking a beer, you are *doing*. When you are watching a movie, you are *doing*. When you are intimate with someone who is not your spouse, you are *doing*. At every turn, with every tick of the clock, whether you are asleep or awake, you are constantly *doing* something. It is the sum total of all your *doing* that is your vocation.

When I ask the question - "What is your vocation?" this is what I am talking about. I am asking you to ask yourself what you are literally doing at that very moment. Every action in your life either draws you closer to God or drives you further from Him. There is no such thing as a neutral action. We tend to think there is, but this is self-deception. Every thing you do is either a step down the path of Plan A or Plan B. It's either a part of God's perfect will for your life or God's permissive will.

So, what are you doing right now?

NOTE:
1. Demarest, *The Cross and Salvation*, 36-37. *Council of Trent*, chapter V-VI. See also Sam Storms, 'The Order of Salvation: Part One', *Enjoying God Ministries*: http://www.enjoyinggodministries.com/article/the-order-of-salvation-part-i/ Retrieved 15 November 2010.

CHAPTER 7 –
TAKE THIS JOB AND SHOVE IT

I was not a very good student when I was in college. Oh, I got mostly As and Bs (and an occasional C), but my GPA could have been so much better had I applied myself and worked toward my potential. But I was content for an A or a B, doing as little work as necessary.

My biggest problem in college was procrastination. I simply put off my class projects and studying for as long as possible. I would literally wait until the very last minute in many cases. This had worked for me in high school and it sort of worked for me in college. I just loved having fun, doing things other than schoolwork.

College equals freedom, and boy, I really loved my freedom! I loved eating pizza at 10:00 o'clock at night. I loved going to see movies in the afternoon. I loved just hanging out in the dorm room of my friends doing nothing at all. I loved everything about college life, except the school work! It's not that I hated school, don't get me wrong. I've always had a love for education, but my problem was the actual discipline of doing the work.

As I said, my biggest problem was procrastination. I just put things off. My professors at OBU would hand us syllabi on the first day of class with all the dates for tests, papers, etc. I knew exactly when everything was due. But rather than plan and prepare, I played. "I'll do it tomorrow," was my motto. So I would find myself the night before a big test cramming and sweating and worrying and wishing I had started earlier. But somehow I got through. Did I learn my lesson? No! I'd do it all again the next time a test rolled around.

As a theology student, I was required to write a lot of papers. Almost every class I took in my major required one big research paper due in the second half of the semester. Would I use my time wisely and collect research throughout the semester? Would I write rough drafts and build the paper over the course of weeks? Nope. I would wait until the last possible moment. Usually the week the paper was due, I'd run to the library and pull sources from the shelves. I would read and digest them as quickly as possible. Then I'd try to hammer out ten pages in just a couple of days.

I got pretty good with this last minute routine. In fact, I got so good at it that I decided I could push the envelope. I wanted to see how far I could take this procrastination thing! I eventually got so good that I could hammer out a full ten-page paper the night before it was due. I'm not saying it was the best work of scholarship, but from my perspective, it got the job done. However, even then I was not satisfied. By the time I was a senior, my habits had degenerated into waiting until the day a paper was due to write it. How did I get away with this? Well, technically, a paper was not considered late until the "end of the day." That was 5:00 p.m. when the office buildings on campus would close and be locked. On the day a paper was due, I'd just dump all my classes and holed up in my on-campus apartment and spend the whole day writing. I actually lived in a second floor unit and outside my bedroom window was a flat roof with rocks on it. My roommates and I used to call it Pebble Beach, and we spent our weekend days out there, soaking up the sun, listening to music, and drinking lemonade. It was great.

On the day a paper was due, I'd set up a small table out on Pebble Beach, run an extension cord to my Smith-Corona typewriter, throw off my t-shirt, and spend the day hammering away. If I needed to run to the library for just one more source, I was about a 60 second dash away. I usually found myself sprinting to Owens Hall, where my professors officed, just in time to beat the 5:00 p.m. deadline. I'd bolt through the front door, slide the paper under my profs office door, and wave bye to the janitor on my way out as he locked the building behind me.

I had perfected the art of procrastinated paper writing!

But there was a price to pay as well. As a result of my choices, I had missed a whole day's worth of classes. Ah well, just more procrastination.

I want you to know that I am in no way advocating this as a method of sound academic achievement in college. In fact, today I am embarrassed that I allowed my study and writing habits to degenerate into what was really a mess. Yes, a mess. I was miserable. The whole time I was putting off my work, I was thinking and worrying about it. It wasn't as if I was truly enjoying myself.

One semester I made a huge mistake with my schedule, which just added to my misery. I decided to take only classes that met after lunch time. You know how college life is - things don't really begin until after 10:00 p.m. It's not unusual at all to be up until after 2:00 a.m., and I loved my sleep when I was younger. By my way of thinking, why kill myself to get up for an 8:00 a.m. class, or even a 9:00 a.m.

class, when the same class is offered at 1:00 p.m.? I can stay up as late (or early) as I want and get all the sleep I want.

As I said, this was a huge mistake. All my friends, and I mean *all*, took morning classes; occasionally one of them would have maybe one afternoon class. Because of this, I would wake up late in the morning to an empty apartment. I'd eat lunch alone. By the time I was getting ready to head out to *start* my day, my roommates and friends were finishing their classes! That's right, they were done. While I was sitting in afternoon classes day after day, I'd be watching out the windows as my friends were throwing the Frisbee or playing football. I'd come back from classes late in the afternoon and listen to them talk about the matinee movie they all went to see that day. Man, I was missing out! I never took all afternoon classes again.

So, what was my problem in college? I don't want to paint a picture that I was a slug or anything. I was overall a pretty good and normal college kid. But I had some really bad habits that grew and grew and eventually led to a lot of unnecessary misery.

Looking back on this time in my life from my current perspective, it's easy for me to see that my whole problem had to do with *vocation*. My fixation was pretty much right on. I was in college to prepare for the ministry. I had great professors, a solid degree plan, and friends that loved the Lord. My location was also where it needed to be. I was attending Oklahoma Baptist University and living on campus. OBU is a great school and without a doubt God led me there.

My problem was narrowed down to one of vocation. I was not doing the right things all the time. My vocation was to be a student and to be the best student I could be. My preparation at OBU would lay the foundation for a lifetime of ministry effectiveness. But I was not always doing what

I needed to be doing. I was not disciplined with my time. Instead of heading out to a movie the night before a major exam that I had not yet studied for, I should have asked, "What is my vocation?" "What should I be doing right now?" The answer was easy, but like Jonah, I headed in the wrong direction. When I was facing a ten page research paper with the knowledge that it was due in three weeks, I should have been *doing* more to prepare for and write that paper. My lack of doing the right things led to misplaced geography, like skipping classes and going places to have fun instead of taking care of business.

I did learn my lesson. In spite of myself, I graduated with a solid GPA and was able to eventually enroll at Southwestern Baptist Theological Seminary to work on my graduate degree. By that time I was married and would go on to have two children while in seminary. I became a very serious student and learned to discipline my habits and my schedule. By the time I was working on my doctorate at Southern Seminary in Louisville, Kentucky, I was a straight-A student.

It was all about getting my vocation right.

I have shared just part of my story to illustrate a point about how vocation works in life. But everyone's life is different. Your story is not the same as mine. It is unique. And we can learn from one another's stories. We can learn the proper paths to follow and we can learn roads not to take.

I want to share with you the vocational story of two men. Both of these men crossed paths in life and at times even walked the same path. But these men were very different from each other. In fact, outside of Jesus Christ, they would have had nothing in common at all. Their stories are found in the New Testament and you probably already know something about each of them. The names of these two men are Paul and Peter.

PAUL

Before there was Paul, there was Saul.

Our first picture of Saul is found in the book of Acts. He is standing by, watching the impromptu execution of a Christian named Stephen. Stephen's crime? Preaching Jesus. Stephen had recently been chosen as one of the first seven to a new office in the early church - the office of deacon. He took pressure off of the original disciples so that they could busy themselves with prayer and the ministry of the Word (Acts 6:4). But Stephen was quite a preacher himself. The Bible records that Stephen was the first, other than the apostles, who was given the power to perform miracles.

In Acts 6, we find Stephen engaged in Jerusalem with a group of fellow Jews from the Synagogue of Freedmen. This synagogue was made up of people who were not native to Israel, many of whom were probably former slaves. Its membership would have included people from northern Africa and the Asian Diaspora, a scattering of Jews to Asia seeking to return to their homeland. It is likely that Saul, being from Cilicia, would have been a member of this particular synagogue as well.[1]

Stephen preached a lengthy sermon to the synagogue, giving them, including the priests, a lesson in Jewish history, and then accusing them of "murdering" the Messiah, sent by God. This enraged the people to the point of frenzy. The text records that the people were so mad that they "ground their teeth." Stephen was thrown out of the synagogue, then out of the city, and stoned by the mob.

I've always thought death by stoning would be one of the most horrible deaths imaginable. To be surrounded by angry faces and then pelted by rocks, one after another, relentlessly...until you die. This is extreme brutality.

I said earlier that Saul was standing by while the stoning of Stephen occurred, but that is not altogether accurate. The Scripture says it this way:

Acts 7:58
Then they cast him (Stephen) out of the city and stoned him. And the witnesses laid down their garments at the feet of a young man named Saul.

This is our introduction to Saul. He was a young man watching over the coats and jackets of those throwing the stones at Stephen. Why would Saul be chosen to keep the coats? Why was he not throwing stones himself? Even though he was still a young man, it seems clear that Saul was a man of authority. The people may have even viewed him as the man in charge.

When you jump down just a few more verses to chapter eight of Acts, you see that Saul may have been the one to "pull the lever" so to speak, on Stephen.

Acts 8:1–3
And Saul approved of his execution. And there arose on that day a great persecution against the church in Jerusalem, and they were all scattered throughout the regions of Judea and Samaria, except the apostles. Devout men buried Stephen and made great lamentation over him. But Saul was ravaging the church, and entering house after house, he dragged off men and women and committed them to prison.

Saul is directly tied to the "great persecution" of Christians throughout Jerusalem and then later the whole region. He is depicted as the ring-leader. The imagery is even more graphic in verse three when we are told that Saul "ravaged the church." There was a witch hunt underway and Saul was at the helm, driving the hunt.

What was Saul's vocation? Christian killer.

How did this happen? Is there any scenario where this would be acceptable even within the strict laws of Judaism? We have seen in just a few verses a brutal picture of Saul, but who he was and how he got that way requires more information.

Saul was born into a proud Jewish family that lived in Tarsus of Cilicia. This was a heavily Roman province and Saul was, in fact, also a Roman citizen. As a Jew he was of the tribe of Benjamin and his dual citizenship would serve him well as a killer of Christians, providing access and immunity. Not much else is known about Saul's family, other than that he did have at least one sister and a nephew (Acts 23:16).

Saul was a devout Jew, and living in Tarsus would not have afforded him much of an opportunity for a good Jewish education. So Saul moved to Jerusalem, probably while still a child. Once there, we know from his own testimony that he studied under the tutelage of the great Jewish Rabbi Gamaliel (Acts 22:3). Knowing that Saul was a student of Gamaliel is significant. Gamaliel was a very prominent rabbi, and the grandson of one of the greatest rabbis in all of Jewish history, Rabbi Hillel.

Each rabbi was known for the particular way they interpreted the Law and the Prophets (the Old Testament for Christians). Very bright male Jewish students would hope to be chosen by a rabbi whose theology most closely matched their own. Of course, among rabbis there was a pecking order, with some being more highly regarded than others. At the time of Christ, the two most prominent and competing rabbis were Hillel and Shammai. The School of Hillel was considered to be more liberal, while the School of

Shammai was conservative, this from a Jewish theological perspective.

Both the Schools of Hillel and Shammai were on the pharisaical side of the continuum. The School of Hillel would eventually become the more popular of the two, and Hillel's teachings would go on to be a part of the Jewish Talmudical writings even to this day.[2]

Knowing that Saul was a student of Gamaliel means that he was of the School of Hillel, arguably the most prominent rabbi of all time. No doubt that Saul was a Jew among Jews. He was pure and devoted. Saul did not have a fixation problem. I believe, more than most, he was fixated on God, wanting to do anything and everything he could to serve God. Even if it meant killing Christians who he thought perverted Judaism.

But everything changed for Saul one day while he was traveling to the city of Damascus. The reason for his journey was to continue the hunt. Look at what the text tells us:

Acts 9:1–2

But Saul, still breathing threats and murder against the disciples of the Lord, went to the high priest and asked him for letters to the synagogues at Damascus, so that if he found any belonging to the Way, men or women, he might bring them bound to Jerusalem.

His fixation was clear – Judaism. His location was Jerusalem, headed to Damascus. His vocation was a hunt for Christians. But while on the road to Damascus, Saul had an encounter. A bright light from heaven flashed, knocking Saul off his animal and to the ground. What kind of light this was is uncertain, but I would guess it was something like a lightening strike. When I was a Boy Scout, I was camping with my troop once when a lightning bolt struck our campsite. It blew me onto my back and I could instantly taste sulfur in my mouth. Very weird and very powerful.

I think something similar but more intense happened to Saul. The power of lightning knocked him flat. Then Saul heard the voice, "Saul, why are you persecuting me?" Unsure of who was speaking to him and what this voice wanted, Saul inquired, "Who are you Lord?" The word *Lord* used here was a term of respect and not one of divinity. Then came the reply, and I am sure that the following words knocked Saul's soul to the ground to join his body:

Acts 9:5–6
And he said, "I am Jesus, whom you are persecuting. But rise and enter the city, and you will be told what you are to do."

I think the choice of Jesus' words to Saul is very interesting. He wants Saul to go on to the city of Damascus and wait for instruction on "what you are to *do*." In one reply we get it all, a new fixation: Jesus. A location: Damascus. And a vocation: a promise of something to *do*.

You may know the rest of the story of Saul. He would go on to profess Jesus. This in turn led to him being hunted with a price on his own head. Saul would find it difficult to have friends anywhere. The Jews wanted to kill him for becoming a Christian, and Christians didn't want to have anything to do with him for fear that it was all a trick to root them out. Saul would spend three years in exile and then return as Paul, the missionary. He would go on to become the most prominent leader of the early church, and would eventually pen the majority of the New Testament.

As you can see, Jesus had a lot in mind when he told Saul to wait for instructions on what he wanted him to do!

PETER

Paul had a counterpart in the ministry. His name was Peter. Yes, this is the same Peter that was one of the original 12 disciples. Peter followed the same *Ordo Salutis* as Paul in working out his salvation, but Peter's story is radically different from Paul's, illustrating how God works in a unique way in each of our lives.

Whereas Paul was highly educated, Peter was uneducated. Paul came from a wealthy family and Peter came from a poor family. Paul grew up in a town in the center of Roman influence, Peter grew up in a rural village off the beaten path. Paul was controlled, and Peter, at times, out of control. Paul's ministry would be to the Gentiles and Peter's ministry would be to the Jews. Paul would be the patriarch of the church abroad, and Peter the patriarch of the church in Jerusalem. Paul would write over half the New Testament, Peter would only write eight chapters. Both men would die at the hand of Nero.

The opposite, but the same.

From different worlds, but of the same Kingdom.

Nothing in common, but Jesus in common.

That's Paul and Peter, and Peter's story is every bit as fascinating as Paul's. Peter's story begins in similar fashion as Paul's. He too was known by another name before being known as Peter. That name was Simon.

Simon didn't do very well in school. He was not a good student. His Greek was not the best and his command of the Torah was not exceptional. How do I know this? Because when we first see Simon, he is fishing.

Matthew 4:18

While walking by the Sea of Galilee, he saw two brothers, Simon (who is called Peter) and Andrew his brother, casting a net into the sea, for they were fishermen.

Here we have what appears to be a normal day by the Sea of Galilee. The Sea of Galilee is located in extreme northern Israel, and at the time of Jesus it was surrounded by numerous small fishing villages. Jesus himself grew up about ten miles to the west of the Sea of Galilee in Nazareth.

On this particular day, Jesus is walking along the shore of the Sea of Galilee and he sees two brothers fishing, Simon and Andrew. In order to understand and appreciate Simon's story, we must ask and answer a very important question - why were they fishing? Too many times we read so quickly through the Bible without stopping to look at the obvious. Two brothers are fishing. Why? The easy answer is that they are hungry and they are either fishing to eat or to sell for an income. But the question I am asking is deeper than this surface answer. Let me rephrase: why are they fishermen? To answer that question you must first understand how the Jewish education system worked.

BETH-SEPHER

Around the age of six, all Jewish children would go to a Jewish school, much in the same way we send our kids to school today around the same age. The first of these schools was called *Beth-Sepher*, which means House of the Book. Virtually the entire Jewish education curriculum centered around the Torah: reading, studying, interpreting and memorizing the text.

Taught by rabbis, the goal was to lead the students to view the Word of God as much more than mere words on a scroll. Just like today, students had their own version of school supplies, and on the first day of class, each student would take their slate and be instructed by the rabbi to smear honey all over it. The students would then lick the honey off the slate while the rabbi would say the words, "May you never forget that the words of God are like honey."

This had a powerful impact on the Jewish children. They learned at a very young age to equate the Word of God as sweetness on the tongue. The children would link the study of God's Word in a very experiential way with one of the most pleasurable delicacies of the day, honey. All of a sudden Psalm 34:8 explodes to life when it instructs us to, "Taste and see that the Lord is good." Is this how you feel about the Bible?

The children would begin their studies by memorizing the Torah. *Beth-Sepher* would last until age ten, when the entire Torah would be committed to memory. That's right, the whole Torah, the entirety of the first five books of the Bible: Genesis, Exodus, Leviticus, Numbers, and Deuteronomy. This is shocking to most of us today. We do good to memorize a few verses for our own encouragement, or to share with a lost friend. It stretches believability to consider grade school children memorizing whole books of the Bible. How is this possible? Have you ever seen a kid who didn't want to eat their entire bag of Halloween candy the same night they collected it? When you equate the Word of God with the sweetness of candy, kids will gobble it up!

BETH-TALMUD

Not everyone was allowed to move on to the next school, *Beth-Talmud*. Only the best of the best from *Beth-Sepher* were selected to go further with their studies. Lasting until the age of 14, the goal of *Beth-Talmud* was the memorization of the rest of the Hebrew Scriptures. You heard me, the whole Bible. For the Jew, that would be Genesis to Malachi. Once again, this may strike you as impossible, especially since we are talking about teenagers. But this is not impossible. Far from it. I don't know about you, but the teenagers I know have amazing memories. They can quote the lyrics of songs from whole albums, and it is not uncommon to get two 14 year-old-boys together and watch in amazement as they quote, word-for-word the entirety of the movie *Dumb and Dumber*! So yes, with the proper focus and motivation, memorization of God's Word was not only doable but expected for students of *Beth-Talmud*.

Another feature of *Beth-Talmud* was its interactive nature. This highlights an important element of Jewish education. As an example, a rabbi might ask a student, "What is 4+4?" Instead of responding with the answer of eight, the student would respond with, "What is 16 divided by 2?" Do you see what is happening here? Instead of just teaching the kids to spew out answers to questions, the rabbis taught the children to take the information, interact with it, and then give it back to the rabbi in a new form, thus taking the discussion further. Think with me for a minute - how many times in the New Testament do we see Jesus answering a question with a question? This is how Jews interact, and they learn this in *Beth-Talmud*.

Remember the story from Luke 2 when Jesus was 12 years old? His parents and their whole clan had traveled to Jerusalem for Passover, and when they left for home they inadvertently left Jesus behind. Realizing he was not with them, they rushed back to the city to find him. Here is what the Scripture records:

Luke 2:46–47
After three days they found him in the temple, sitting among the teachers, listening to them and asking them questions. And all who heard him were amazed at his understanding and his answers.

Why is Jesus listening to them and asking questions? Because he would have been in *Beth-Talmud*! And then notice that the rabbis and others were amazed at how advanced Jesus was for just being in *Beth-Talmud*, for he had not yet made it to the final school in the Jewish education system.

BETH-MIDRASH

If you made it through *Beth-Talmud*, were one of the best of the best, and were a male, then you would qualify to go on to the final school, *Beth-Midrash*. Lasting from the age of around 14 up until "graduation," this school was for the brightest Jewish young men who would go on to become rabbis themselves.

Beth-Midrash involved a mutual selection process between the student and the rabbi. Each rabbi had their own particular way or flavor of interpreting the Word of God. Some rabbis were more popular and influential than others. For a student to enter *Beth-Midrash*, he must select a rabbi that he wanted to follow, whose teachings and interpretations of God's Word most closely lined up with his own. The teaching of a rabbi was called his "yoke." When a young man was accepted under the tutelage of a rabbi, it was said that he would take the yoke of that rabbi upon himself. You might recall that Jesus, in the book of Matthew, encouraged his followers by telling them that his "yoke was easy and my burden is light" (Matthew 11:30).

As I said, however, the selection process had to be mutual. Once a young man had selected a rabbi whose yoke he wanted to take, he had to prove himself worthy to the rabbi. The rabbi was the one that really held all the cards. The prospective student would approach the rabbi and say something along the lines of, "I want to be your Talmid." The word Talmid means disciple. Each rabbi would have a group of disciples that followed him that he called his Talmidim. A rabbi was very careful about who he accepted as a Talmid, or disciple, because the student would one day go on to represent that rabbi and his teachings. He was responsible for carrying on the "yoke" of that rabbi. The rabbi was looking for young men that he considered worthy.

When a prospective student would approach a rabbi and ask to be his Talmid, an interview process of sorts would be initiated. The rabbi would test the young man to see how well he knew God's Word. He might ask for the teen to consider the book of Habakkuk and to recite verbatim the 17 references to the book of Deuteronomy…and to do it backwards!

There was another technique that rabbis used to test prospective students called the Remez. Here is how the Remez would work. The rabbi would ask the young man a question about a verse in the Bible, but the nature of the question would indicate that what the rabbi was really referring to was the verse either before or after the one being quoted. If the student was good enough, he would recognize this and respond with his own question, quoting a verse, but referring actually to another verse on either side of the one he quoted. This game of mental gymnastics would go on until the rabbi had enough.

The whole point of the Remez was for the rabbi to determine if the young man standing before him had what it took to be his disciple. Was he good enough to carry the yoke of the rabbi and to perpetuate that yoke in the future? If the young man proved himself worthy, he would be accepted into *Beth-Midrash*, become a Talmid, and go on to one day be a rabbi himself. The rabbi would look at the teen and say the words, "Come follow me." This was the dream of all Jewish boys.

To hear these words.

To be a rabbi.

If, however, the rabbi found that the young man was not worthy, he would send him away. What then? What would become of Jewish boys who were not good enough to move on and become rabbis? The answer to that question is obvious. They would go back home to their families. Most families had some sort of business or trade. These Jewish boys would simply learn the family trade and grow up to be an "average Joe."

So let's jump back to our normal ordinary day, to these two brothers fishing by the Sea of Galilee. Remember my question? Why are they fishing? The answer should be easy now. Simon and Andrew are fishing because they aren't good enough. They've been rejected. Somewhere along the way it was determined that they did not have what it took to be rabbis. So they were sent away, dreams dashed, to learn the family trade of fishing and to eke out a living for the rest of their days. That is Simon's vocation. He is a fisherman. He is second tier. He is a reject.

But this ordinary day was far from ordinary. A rabbi is walking along the shore on this day, and not just any rabbi, but Jesus. The same Jesus, that at age 12, blew away the greatest teachers in Jerusalem at his command of God's Word. This Rabbi Jesus is looking for Talmid. Men who have what it takes to follow him, to learn from him, to carry his yoke, and to perpetuate that yoke to future generations.

Jesus sees two young men fishing, but he sees something more. He walks up to Simon and Andrew and utters the words of a rabbi.

Matthew 4:19–20
And he said to them, "Follow me, and I will make you fishers of men." Immediately they left their nets and followed him.

I often wonder at the reaction of Simon and his brother. I mean, think about it. Two guys, minding their own business, plying their trade. Two guys fishing. Along comes a total stranger and he says, "Hey guys, come follow me." And they actually do it?! Who does this? Would you do this? But when you see this scene in context, it all makes perfect sense. This is not just some stranger, this is a rabbi. And

Simon is not just a fisherman, he is a man with shattered dreams. Dreams to be and do so much more, to make a difference in the world. But he's been judged and found wanting. That is until the rabbi comes to him.

What would lead a man to throw down his net, the tools of his trade, and follow Jesus? Because Rabbi Jesus thinks he's got what it takes. He thinks Simon can do it. He thinks that Simon is good enough to carry the yoke and to pass it on. He has tested Simon in some way that only a rabbi knows, and Simon has passed. He is being asked to follow the rabbi! The ultimate dream of a Jewish man has fallen at the feet of Simon. This is his chance, perhaps his only chance, and what does he do? He takes it. "Immediately" is what the Bible says.

In an instant, Jesus changes Simon's vocation. Just like Paul, he would change Simon's name as well. *Petros*, Peter, would be his new name. It means "the rock." That is what Peter would go on to be - "Rocky." Rough around the edges, but so much potential. Fixation and location would never be an issue for Peter. He would get the vocation thing messed up though. During the three years that he followed Rabbi Jesus in the flesh, he was always *doing* the wrong things. Shooting off at the mouth, drawing the sword, denying he knew the Rabbi.

Peter was working out his salvation, the *Ordo Salutis*. Perhaps more than any other of Jesus' Talmidim, you can see the progress so clearly with Peter. In the end, even getting his vocation right was not a problem for Peter. He would be the one that would stand on the day of Pentecost and preach to the masses, convincing 3,000 others to follow the Rabbi. He would become the one that everyone else looked to for leadership as the early church exploded with growth. He would be the one that Paul would come to after his own conversion. He would be the one, this uneducated former fisherman, who would pen two books of the Bible, and most believe he provided the bulk of the material for Mark's gospel. He would be the one that would travel to Rome, the seat of world power, to encourage the persecuted church. And he would be the one that would hang from a cross in Rome, far, far away from the Sea of Galiliee...and die.

Just like the Rabbi that he followed.

FINDING YOU

What about you? Who are you? Where are you? What are you doing? Do you relate to Paul or Peter? I chose to tell the story of these two great fathers of the faith because they represent a spectrum of sorts. Paul is on one end: educated, righteous, wealthy, political. Peter is on the other end: uneducated, common, poor, no one. Apart from Jesus, these men would never have been friends. Because of Jesus they became not only friends, but champions of the faith, whose influence has filtered into the life of every Christian for the last 2,000 years. Each of these men followed the same path, *Ordo Salutis*, working out their salvation. But that path was not cookie-cutter by any means. It was a customized working of God's Holy Spirit in the life of each man.

This is how God works.

This is how he orders our vocation.

So where do you find yourself on the spectrum? Are you more like Paul or Peter? Or are you somewhere in the middle? I can see flashes of both men in my own life. I have had the privilege of one of the best educations in the country, but I did not come from a family of high means or influence - my father was an over-the-road truck driver. I grew up in the relatively ordinary town of Fort Smith, not some metropolitan area like Dallas. I have had the opportunity to travel the world doing work for the Kingdom of God, but given my preference, I'd rather couch-up and read a good book or watch a movie.

I am both Paul and Peter, and I am neither. I am Jeff Crawford. While I walk the same *Ordo Salutis* as all other believers before me, God is doing something different and unique in my life that He has not done in anyone else's life before. I find that exhilarating. I know that God loves me and wants the best for me. He also has an end product He is shooting for with me, and He is going to put me in locations with certain vocations to accomplish in order to get me there.

I wonder sometimes what my vocation would have been had I not found Jesus. Had he not found me, not walked up to me, and changed my life forever by uttering those words in my ear, "Come follow me." What would have happened had I not followed? Where would I be today? What would I be fixated on? What would I be doing? Right now, this very minute. I may not know the answer to all of those questions but this I do know…I would be lost. In finding Jesus, I really found myself.

What about you?

Have you found yourself?

NOTES:

1. Polhil, James. *The New American Commentary: Acts.* Broadman Press: Nashville, TN. 1992, page 84.

2. To read more on the Schools of Hillel and Shammai see: Douglas, J.D. and Philip W. Comfort, eds. *Who's Who in Christian History.* Tyndale House Publisher: Wheaton, Il. 1992. And Cross, F.L., ed. *The Oxford Dictionary of the Christian Church: Revised Third Edition*, edited by E.A. Livingston. Oxford University Press. Oxford, UK. 2005.

CHAPTER 8 –
COURSE CORRECTIONS

I've talked a lot about Plan A and Plan B in the pages of this book. God has a definite and unique plan for your life. A plan that is designed to bless you and not harm you, to give you a hope and a future (Jeremiah 29:11). This God plan is what I have called Plan A for your life. It is God's perfect will for you. You also have God's permissive will, the choices He allows you to make in your life that deviate from Plan A. This plan, which is really a plan of your own making, is Plan B.

We have looked at the consequences of choosing Plan B. We have seen what Jonah endured because of his Plan B choices, and the negative impact it had on the lives of other people, the Domino Effect. It is my hope and prayer that you have determined to pursue God's will for your life, not His permissive will, but His perfect will, Plan A. I have given you a powerful tool to stay on course with God's Plan A. It is the principle of triangulation as determined by answering three simple questions:

What is my fixation?

What is my location?

What is my vocation?

These three questions are it. They are the key to knowing, almost intuitively, what Plan A is for your life. I am convinced that as you walk through the day-to-day routine of life, constantly coming back to these questions, they will function as a safeguard to keep you from running off the rails. It may seem mechanical at first, to ask yourself these questions, but my experience is that the more you practice and ask them, the more natural they become, to the point that you eventually won't even think about them.

You must use the principle of triangulation in your life with the little things, the details. This is where most people go wrong. They try to live their lives the way they want to in the "little" things, the things they think are unimportant. They want Plan B for the day-to-day routine of life, and they want Plan A for only the big things, those major crossroads in life. But God just does not work that way. If you are living life on your terms regarding all the small things, when you come to the major crossroads of life, you will be lost. God will seem far away and you won't have a clue which way to go. But if you choose Plan A, God's perfect will, for everything in life, then the big stuff won't even seem like big stuff. You will just know. That is ultimately the goal of this book, to help people know how to find God's perfect will for their lives.

We have seen this principle of triangulation and all three questions played out in the real life story of Jonah. We have watched as his fixation, location, and vocation got all out of whack. And we have watched the consequences to Jonah and to those around him. Running from Plan A can have devastating consequences in life. I believe that the turmoil, the evil and suffering that we see dominating this world, is directly linked to people choosing Plan B on a massive scale. You may not be able to control what others do with God's will, but you can control what you do, which Plan you choose.

In this final chapter, I want to address something related to all this talk of Plan A and Plan B that you may have been thinking the whole way through. Somewhere along the way, while reading these pages, you may have asked yourself, "What do I do if I discover that I have been following Plan B? Have I blown it? Have I gone too far and missed any hope of ever getting back to Plan A, back on God's track?" That is a great question and something you actually *should* have been asking yourself and God.

I am so happy to be able to tell you that, because God is all-knowing and all-seeing and all-powerful, He always provides a way back. You can never go so far that God can't or won't provide for course corrections. Now that is not to say that the road back will be easy. Sometimes we have to sleep in the bed we make.

And that is exactly what we see with Jonah...

JONAH'S SALVATION

When we last left Jonah, he had finally come to the end of himself. His fixation was all messed up - he was focused on himself and on running from God. His location was all wrong - he was on a ship to Tarshish, headed in the exact opposite direction from where he needed to go. And his vocation was out of whack - he was doing all the wrong things. Instead of preaching, he was hanging with a bunch of sailors, bragging about how he could outrun God.

Then came the storm. Not just any storm, but the perfect storm; one that would sink the boat and doom all those on board. Because Jonah was so far off course, he had no idea that things were as bad as they were and certainly didn't know it was his fault. All that changed as the frantic crew pulled him topside to face the storm of his making. It became clear to all, even Jonah, that he was the culprit. His choices had led to this point of desperation.

Jonah finally got the message.

He realized that it was up to him to find a solution.

Jonah 1:11–12

Then they said to him (Jonah), "What shall we do to you, that the sea may quiet down for us?" For the sea grew more and more tempestuous. He said to them, "Pick me up and hurl me into the sea; then the sea will quiet down for you, for I know it is because of me that this great tempest has come upon you."

Many of those who have studied the story of Jonah have proposed that Jonah came to the end of himself while inside the belly of the whale. That while he was in the whale he finally gave in to God and repented. I don't see that. I think Jonah's "conversion" happened in verses 11 and 12 of chapter one. This is where we see Jonah owning this mess. He knows it is all his fault. This is where we see repentance, not in the whale, but on board the ship in the midst of the storm.

Repentance is when you stop doing wrong and start doing right. The picture of repentance is a 180-degree turnaround. Too many times we only go halfway with repentance, we just stop doing the wrong. We never start doing the right. When you only quit doing wrong, it's not real, biblical repentance. It just means you're tired and want to rest. Biblical repentance requires walking back from where you came, and that usually means hard work and lots of it.

That is what we see from Jonah in this passage. He is ready to repent. He is done with Tarshish and the boat and all the turmoil that his Plan B has caused everyone. There is something here I want to point out that I think is easily missed. I think Jonah believed he had blown it. I mean blown it permanently. I think that standing there on that ship, pounded by the waves and the rain and the wind, Jonah came to a realization of what Plan B had really gotten him, and he just knew in his spirit that there was no way back.

Have you ever felt that way? Have you ever felt like you've walked so far away from God that there is no way back? Your fixation has been on everything *but* God. You're constantly in places and locations where you don't belong, and you are never where you do belong. The things you do, the vocations you undertake, are things that you never thought someone like you would ever be involved in. That is your life…and Plan A seems so far away, like a lost dream that can never be recovered.

That is exactly what I think Jonah was feeling. But what Jonah did next made all the difference in the world. Instead of just giving up and resigning himself to finishing his Plan B no matter the cost to himself or others, Jonah chose to repent. If he was going to die, then he was going to die taking a step toward God and not away from Him.

Don't miss this because I think it is vitally important. Too many people never take a step back toward God, they never repent, because they think they've gone too far. My friend, there is no such thing as too far for God. You must hold on to that and believe that.

I think Jonah believed that death was inevitable. I mean, think about it, he is asking to be tossed overboard. Now that's a change in location! It's the one thing he can do to get back on track with God before he dies. Tarshish is this way, Nineveh is that way. "Throw me overboard, boys! At least I'll die a step closer to where I was supposed to be than if I stay here. And don't worry, once I'm gone, God will take care of you."

So over the side he went, and sure enough, the storm abated. But what about Jonah, what happened to him? Like I said, I firmly believe Jonah thought this was the end.

Think with me for a moment - what are his options, really? If someone tossed you overboard in the middle of the ocean, even without a storm, what do you think your fate would be? Jonah had no thoughts other than "this is it." He was done for and Plan A was lost forever.

But that is not how God works. God always provides a way back. And in Jonah's case the way back, his salvation, was a really big fish.

JONAH AND THE WHALE

This is the most famous part about the Jonah story. This is the part my youngest son loves! Jonah gets swallowed up by a whale. The Bible actually says a "great fish," but you get the idea. The whole Jonah and the whale scene is so out of the ordinary, so novel, so unbelievable, that we tend to not consider the human drama unfolding. I mean, what if *you* were swallowed by a whale? How bad would that be?! The answer is BAD! Maybe not as bad as dying, but this is bad. A miracle for sure, but not exactly first-class accommodations back to the mainland.

The belly of a whale would be a torturous place. Stomach acids would work on digesting your flesh. The stench of seaweed, sea water, rotten fish, etc. would be overwhelming. There would be times when breathable air would be limited as the fish surfaced and dove again. And then the darkness, the lost sense of time. The pressure of the deep. The not knowing if you would die here, be spit back out into the ocean, or something worse. The thought of actually making it out alive and back to land would have been too good to consider. It would have been natural for Jonah to think that this was just prolonging the inevitable. But that is not what Jonah thought. We know this because we have a record of what happened next in Jonah's own words.

Jonah 2:1-9

*Then Jonah prayed to the L*ORD *his God from the belly of the fish, saying,*

> *"I called out to the L*ORD, *out of my distress,*
> *and he answered me;*
> *out of the belly of Sheol I cried,*
> *and you heard my voice.*
> *For you cast me into the deep,*
> *into the heart of the seas,*
> *and the flood surrounded me;*
> *all your waves and your billows*
> *passed over me.*
> *Then I said, 'I am driven away*
> *from your sight;*
> *yet I shall again look*
> *upon your holy temple.'*
> *The waters closed in over me to take my life;*
> *the deep surrounded me;*
> *weeds were wrapped about my head*
> *at the roots of the mountains.*
> *I went down to the land*
> *whose bars closed upon me forever;*
> *yet you brought up my life from the pit,*
> *O L*ORD *my God.*
> *When my life was fainting away,*
> *I remembered the L*ORD,
> *and my prayer came to you,*
> *into your holy temple.*
> *Those who pay regard to vain idols*
> *forsake their hope of steadfast love.*
> *But I with the voice of thanksgiving*
> *will sacrifice to you;*
> *what I have vowed I will pay.*
> *Salvation belongs to the L*ORD*!"*

Notice what we are told in verse one - "Jonah prayed." This is tremendous. It means that Jonah recovered his fixation on God. A simple change of location (being thrown overboard) led to a change of fixation. What does Jonah do, what does his vocation become? Prayer. Jonah triangulates God's perfect will. Now he is by no means back on track, but he has made some major course corrections. In just a few verses he goes from doing everything wrong to doing everything right.

What I find amazing is that Jonah exalts and praises God in the midst of what he believes are the last moments of his life. This prayer paints a vivid picture. Jonah is sinking into the depths of the ocean. He is dying. It is dark and cold and lonely. "Weeds" are wrapped around his head. Just as his "life was fainting away," Jonah "remembered the LORD." There it is - fixation. Jonah wants his last earthly thought to be filled with God. And so...

He prays.

God hears.

Jonah surrenders.

God saves.

The climax of the prayer is the last sentence - "Salvation belongs to the LORD!"

This can be your story too. God has a way, beyond anything I could ever write or explain, of taking your Plan B mistakes and using them for His Plan A. This is part of what makes your life story unique and makes you who you are. The Bible is right when it says that "all things work together for good" for those who love God and "are called according to his purpose" (Romans 8:28). The words "His purpose" are just another way of saying Plan A. No matter where you are or how far you've traveled, God is right there. Plan A is really only a step away. It may not be an easy step, and it may seem that all is hopeless. But remember Jonah. Remember the storm, and the sea, and remember his prayer. Then remember the whale and remember, most of all, that God saves.

It's time to cast yourself overboard into the arms of God.

A Personal Story

I couldn't wait to graduate. Four years at Oklahoma Baptist University were coming to an end and the rest of my life was in front of me. I had met the girl of my dreams, we were set to be married the month following graduation, and life was good. As my final semester at OBU progressed there were many important decisions to make, like how I was going to make money!

I was at a crossroads and I had options. Which one was Plan A, God's perfect will? One option was to stay in Shawnee and move into married student housing. Julie had one more year left to finish her degree in journalism, and transferring to another school at this point could set her back in no small way. I was serving part-time as the youth pastor of a small church outside of Shawnee and was free to continue there, and I could get another job to supplement my income.

Another option was to move to Fort Worth, Texas and begin my graduate work at Southwestern Baptist Theological Seminary. Most all my ministry friends were either already down there or headed that direction, and I knew that I needed to earn my Master of Divinity degree in order to complete my education and preparation for ministry. Of course we'd have to start from scratch down there in a town we did not know, I'd have to find a job, and Julie would still need to complete school.

A third option was to accept a job offer in Baton Rouge, Louisiana to work on a church growth project. Julie and I were friends with Rick Edmonds, the associate pastor of Parkview Baptist Church. Rick was actually going to be the one performing our wedding and he had offered both Julie and I positions. Combined we would not make much money, but it would be enough. New Orleans Baptist Theological Seminary was an hour away for me and Louisiana State University was in town where Julie could finish her degree.

I didn't know what to do. I can still remember the pressure building as the semester progressed and my time was running out. Remember that I was a big-time procrastinator in college, so all of this together did not put me in a good place or frame of mind. I reached a breaking point one evening. I had to decide. Plans had to be made. My fiancé wanted to know where she was going to live and go to school. It was all on my shoulders. The first real adult decision I would make with other people's lives on the line, and I did not want to mess up.

I went outside my apartment building one evening when it was good and dark and walked around to the side yard where no one could see me. And I broke down. I remember looking up into night sky and staring at the stars. As tears began to flow, I cried out to God to show me the way. "Just give me a sign, God." How many times have you asked God for a sign? I wish I had known then the three questions and the principle of triangulation. But I did not. And I got no sign that night either.

From what I've already shared in previous chapters you probably guessed that I chose option three. We moved to Baton Rouge and took the positions at Parkview. Julie transferred to LSU (amazingly, they took all her hours), and I started part-time enrollment at New Orleans Seminary. Let me tell you what drove my decision, and to this day I am not proud of what I am about to admit. I made my decision based on what I was fixated on, where I wanted to be, and what I wanted to do. The move to Baton Rouge was all about Jeff.

I was tired of school. I didn't want to go to Southwestern and enroll as a full-time student. I wanted a break after four years at OBU. I wanted out of Oklahoma. I had been to Louisiana several times over the previous few years for camps and retreats and really liked the feel of the state. And I wanted to be in the ministry *now*. I didn't want to have to wait any longer. I was prideful and arrogant and just felt that I had what it took and that to wait any longer was a waste of my immense talent and skill. So Baton Rouge it was.

Our first 18 months of marriage were tough. They were hard in so many ways. Yes, we were in love and happy to be married and making it through with lots of laughter, but it was not easy. Carpooling to New Orleans every day to attend seminary classes turned out to be unsustainable. I quit after the first 9-week term. LSU was a different world than OBU. It was a carnal, worldly environment and Julie struggled each and every day she attended class. But she did it because that's the way she is. Once she starts something, she is determined to finish. That is one of the many reasons I love her and why I am a blessed man.

We made very little money. Parkview did everything they said they would do for us financially, but I had underestimated what it would really take to pay for our basic needs as a young married couple. As a result, we began to look for something different after about nine months. I ended up landing a full-time position on the staff of another church in Baton Rouge. It looked great on the surface, but it turned out to be a nightmare. It was, hands down, the worst experience of my ministry. I won't take time to share the details here, but the pastor was a cheat and a crook and working for him was utter misery.

In the midst of all this turmoil, Julie was diagnosed with thyroid cancer and endured surgery and radiation therapy. That too is a whole other story that I won't share here, but suffice it to say that our time in Baton Rouge was not pleasant. I came to the end of myself. In many ways I felt like Jonah. I really wondered if I had blown it. In retrospect, I believe that we should have chosen an option other than moving to Baton Rouge. I think that Baton Rouge was my plan, Plan B. But God let me go anyway. He allowed it within His permissive will. But there was a price to pay, and the road back was not easy.

I remember wondering if I had blown it completely, if I would ever be able to get back on track. That may sound silly to you. You may be measuring my story to your story and thinking that you've blown it much more than I have. But as a young couple in our early 20s with little to no life experience at the time, this hill seemed almost too big to climb. Until Julie and I fixated on God. We cried out to Him and asked Him to deliver us. We offered to change location and vocation if that is what God wanted. Through a crazy set of circumstances, in a two-week period in January of 1994, we went from living life at a dead-end in Baton Rouge, to me sitting in a Hebrew class at Southwestern Seminary in Fort Worth, Texas. Julie had found a full-time job, and we had been assigned the "last" student housing unit on campus. I was enrolled full-time, I had landed a part-time job at a shoe store…and we were right square in the middle of Plan A.

All in two weeks.

Yes, indeed, "Salvation belongs to the LORD!"

ONE STORY – TWO CHARACTERS

Your life is a story. A wonderfully planned, one-of-a-kind story penned by God Himself. The story has two characters, you and God. The marvelous thing about your story is that God lets you hold the pen with Him. He gives you freedom to write the pages. So you have a choice. You can listen to God as He whispers the narrative of your life into your ear and you can apply pen to paper and write. Or you can run from God and write your own story, your own words scribbled onto the parchment. But this story is not just a story to be written and shelved. This story really is your life, and each and every day is a page that must be written.

So what will you write today?

As you look back at the pages that have already been set in stone, you may be ashamed. I know I've got some chapters I wish I could tear out of my story. But I can't... and you can't either.

Here's the wonderful thing about your story - It's not finished! And neither are you. As long as you breathe there is more to write. To rejoin God's story, to recapture His plan for your life, His perfect will, all you have to do is listen to His voice. And ask Him the questions:

"God, am I fixated on you?" And you will know.

"Lord, where should I be...right now?" And you will know.

"Father, what should I be doing?" And you will know.

Remember, knowing and obeying are two vastly different things. Jonah learned the hard way. You learn from Jonah.

By the way, how did things turn out for old Jonah? Did he ever get back to Plan A? As it turned out, the fish really did deliver him back to shore. "Vomited" is the word the Bible uses. Just another lesson for Jonah, I think. Then God had something to say to Jonah.

Jonah 3:1–3
Then the word of the LORD came to Jonah the second time, saying, "Arise, go to Nineveh, that great city, and call out against it the message that I tell you." So Jonah arose and went to Nineveh, according to the word of the LORD.

Sounds a lot like how the whole story of Jonah began in the first place, doesn't it? Except this time Jonah got it right. He inclined his ear to the voice of God. Jonah listened as God began to unfold the story of his life. The story that God, not Jonah, had written. God's perfect will, His Plan A.

Then Jonah applied pen to paper…and wrote.

About the Author

Jeff Crawford, Ed.D., is a pastor, educator, and author. He makes his home in the River Valley of Arkansas with his wife, Julie, and their three children. He is the author of the award winning book, *Image of God – From Who You Are To Who You Can Become*, published by Xulon Press.

9 781615 077793